Challenges to Fiscal Adjustment in Latin America

THE CASES OF ARGENTINA, BRAZIL, CHILE AND MEXICO

Edited by
Luiz de Mello

OECD

ORGANISATION FOR ECONOMIC CO-OPERATION AND DEVELOPMENT

ORGANISATION FOR ECONOMIC CO-OPERATION AND DEVELOPMENT

The OECD is a unique forum where the governments of 30 democracies work together to address the economic, social and environmental challenges of globalisation. The OECD is also at the forefront of efforts to understand and to help governments respond to new developments and concerns, such as corporate governance, the information economy and the challenges of an ageing population. The Organisation provides a setting where governments can compare policy experiences, seek answers to common problems, identify good practice and work to co-ordinate domestic and international policies.

The OECD member countries are: Australia, Austria, Belgium, Canada, the Czech Republic, Denmark, Finland, France, Germany, Greece, Hungary, Iceland, Ireland, Italy, Japan, Korea, Luxembourg, Mexico, the Netherlands, New Zealand, Norway, Poland, Portugal, the Slovak Republic, Spain, Sweden, Switzerland, Turkey, the United Kingdom and the United States. The Commission of the European Communities takes part in the work of the OECD.

OECD Publishing disseminates widely the results of the Organisation's statistics gathering and research on economic, social and environmental issues, as well as the conventions, guidelines and standards agreed by its members.

This work is published on the responsibility of the Secretary-General of the OECD. The opinions expressed and arguments employed herein do not necessarily reflect the official views of the Organisation or of the governments of its member countries.

Foreword

In 1999, the OECD launched the South America Programme with a focus on Argentina, Brazil and Chile. Since then, country surveys have been carried out for Brazil (2001 and 2005) and Chile (2003 and 2005). In addition, a monograph was published in 2004 on the determinants of international competitiveness in South America. The current monograph is based on the proceedings of a conference, hosted by the Economics Department of the OECD on 10 November 2004, on public finances in Latin America at large, with emphasis on Argentina, Brazil, Chile and Mexico.

The time is now ripe for taking stock of developments in public finances in Latin America. The countries that have achieved macroeconomic stability in the region have made considerable progress to put their public finances in order. The perception that fiscal discipline is a pre-requisite for sustained, resilient growth now appears to be well entrenched in those countries. Others are still grappling with the fiscal imbalances, such as chronic budget deficits and high public indebtedness, which have been at the root of macroeconomic disarray in the region during most of the 1980s and early 1990s. Structural reform, including pension reform and the de-regulation of product markets, has underpinned fiscal adjustment. The adoption of rules-based institutional frameworks for monetary and fiscal policymaking has been an additional contributing factor.

But, notwithstanding the achievements of the last 15 years or so, much remains to be done. Of particular importance is the need to consolidate fiscal adjustment, making sure that fiscal effort is conducive to a sustained reduction in public indebtedness so as to allow fiscal policy to play a more stabilising role in the economy. In those countries that are more reliant on natural resources as a source of revenue for the budget, the need to insulate the public finances from volatility in commodity prices remains a challenge. Improving the targeting of government programmes can also do much for public finances to play an effective distributive role in societies that are still faced with a relatively skewed distribution of income.

Jean-Philippe Cotis
Head of the OECD Economics Department

Thanks are due to Anne Legendre and Mee-Lan Frank for statistical and technical assistance.

List of contributors

(In alphabetical order)

José Pablo Arellano is President of the board of *Fundación Chile*, an institution that promotes technological innovation. He has held several senior positions in the Chilean government, including those of Minister of Education and Director of the Budget Office. Mr. Arellano, a graduate from Harvard University, is also a member of the board of several private and public companies, as well as non-profit organisations, including TVN, the leading Chilean television broadcasting corporation, and *Banco del Estado*.

Rogelio Arellano Cadena currently works at the Bank of Mexico and is Professor at the Universidad de las Americas in Mexico. He holds a PhD from the University of California at Los Angeles and has worked extensively on monetary and fiscal issues.

Jorge Braga de Macedo is Professor of Economics at Nova University and President of the Tropical Research Institute, both in Lisbon. He is Research Associate of the National Bureau of Economic Research, Cambridge, MA; and Research Fellow of the Centre for Economic Policy Research, London, England. He has published widely, taught at universities in France and the United States and worked in several international organisations.

Luiz de Mello is Head of the Brazil/South America Desk of the Economics Department of the OECD. Prior to joining the OECD, he held a lectureship at the Economics Department of the University of Kent, United Kingdom, and was a Senior Economist at the Fiscal Affairs Department of the International Monetary Fund. His main interests are public finances and international finance, with emphasis on emerging market economies.

Fausto Hernández-Trillo is Professor at CIDE, an economics research and teaching institution in Mexico, having taught at Ohio State University and

CHALLENGES TO FISCAL ADJUSTMENT IN LATIN AMERICA – ISBN 9264022074 © OECD 2006

the University of Texas. He holds a PhD from Ohio State University and has published numerous articles on financial and fiscal issues.

Fabio Giambiagi is a staff member of the National Economic and Social Development Bank of Brazil (BNDES). He co-authored several books including "*Public Finances: Theory and Practice in Brazil*", "*Economic Reforms in Brazil*" and "*Contemporary Brazilian Economy: 1945/2004*". Mr. Giambiagi worked as a staff member of the Inter-American Development Bank and as an Advisor to the Minister of Planning in the Fernando Henrique Cardoso administration. He currently holds a research position at IPEA, a government think-tank, while on secondment from BNDES.

Pablo Guidotti is Dean of the School of Government and Professor of Economics at the University Torcuato di Tella, Director of Fundación Universidad Torcuato di Tella and Director of LECG, LLC. He is a founding member of the Latin American Shadow Financial Regulatory Committee. Among previous positions in the public and private sectors, Dr. Guidotti has been Deputy Minister of Finance and Secretary of the Treasury of Argentina, Member of the Board of Directors of the Central Bank and Member of the Executive Board for the Trust Fund for Bank Capitalization. He also was Co-Chairman of the G22 Working Group on Strengthening Financial Systems. Dr. Guidotti has published numerous articles in books and journals, and holds a Ph.D. in Economics from the University of Chicago.

Val Koromzay is Director of the Country Studies Branch of the Economics Department of the OECD. He is a graduate of Yale University. After working at the Board of Governors of the Federal Reserve System, he worked at the Council of Economic Advisors in Washington, D.C. He has been at OECD since 1981, in different senior positions. He has worked and written in the areas of economic policy, Balance of Payments, and Central and Eastern Europe economic policies. He now has particular responsibilities with respect to the OECD Economic Surveys of each of the Member countries (and a few non-Member countries) as well as related work published in the OECD's Economic Outlook.

Bénédicte Larre is Head of the Mexico/Portugal Desk of the Economics Department of the OECD. Prior to that, she held various posts in the Economics Department, including on the country desks responsible for Canada, New Zealand, Italy and Switzerland. Ms. Larre is a graduate of the University of Paris II.

Patrick Lenain is Head of Division in the Country Study Branch of the OECD Economics Department, where he contributes to the regular Economic

Surveys of Member countries. Prior to this function, he worked as Economic Counsellor in the office of the OECD's Chief Economist and, before joining the OECD, he occupied various functions at the International Monetary Fund, including the position of Resident Representative to Ukraine. He also had assignments with the Ministry of Finance of France, the European Commission and BAK Basel Economics. He earned his Doctorate in Economics from the University of Paris IX Dauphine.

Juan Carlos Lerda is Professor of public finance and fiscal decentralisation in the Master's programme on public policies and management of the University of Chile. He previously taught at the Department of Economics, University of Brasília, Brazil, and the Faculty of Economic Sciences, National University of Cordoba, Argentina, and was Regional Adviser on Fiscal Policy for Latin America and the Caribbean at the UN Economic Commission for Latin America and the Caribbean (ECLAC). He holds a PhD in Economics from the University of Harvard.

Nanno Mulder is Economist at the Brazil/South-America desk of the Economics Department of the OECD. Before joining OECD, he was a researcher at the Centre for International Economics (CEPII) of the French Planning Agency. The main themes of his research are economic growth and productivity, with a focus on Latin America. Mr. Mulder holds a PhD from the University of Groningen.

Joaquim Oliveira Martins is Principal Economist at the OECD Economics Department, currently heading projects on the economics of ageing, longevity and health systems. He was previously Head of Desk for emerging markets (Brazil, Chile) and several transition countries. He also worked and published on other topics, such as the economics of climate change, product market competion and international competitivess in South America. Previously, he was Research Fellow at CEPII (*Centre d'Etudes Prospectives et d'Informations Internationales*), Paris. He is a lecturer at University of Paris-Dauphine and *Institut d'Études Politiques de Paris*. He holds graduate degrees from the universities of Paris-I and Paris-VI, and *Instituto Comercial de Lisboa*.

Marcio Ronci is Senior Economist at the International Monetary Fund. Previously, he worked as an economist at the European Central Bank, the Brazilian Institute of Economics of the Getúlio Vargas Foundation, and the Brazilian Securities and Exchange Commission of the Ministry of Finance. He holds a PhD in Economics from the Graduate School of Economics, Getúlio Vargas Foundation, and was a visiting researcher at the Department of Economics of the London School of Economics.

CHALLENGES TO FISCAL ADJUSTMENT IN LATIN AMERICA – ISBN 9264022074 © OECD 2006

Lisa M. Schineller is Director in the Sovereign Ratings Group at Standard & Poor's. She is the primary analyst for Brazil and other credits in Latin America. Before joining Standard & Poor's in 1999, Ms. Schineller worked at the International Finance Division of the Federal Reserve Board of Governors, Exxon Company International, and was an Assistant Professor at McGill University. She holds a Ph.D. in economics from Yale University.

Teresa Ter-Minassian is Director of the Fiscal Affairs Department of the International Monetary Fund, having held several senior positions at the IMF, in which capacity she negotiated Stand-By Agreements with Argentina, Brazil and Portugal. She holds degrees in Law from the University of Rome and in Economics from the University of Harvard. She also headed the IMF Task Force for the joint study of the Soviet economy, commissioned to the IMF, IBRD, OECD and EBRD by the G7. Mrs. Ter-Minassian's areas of principal interest and expertise include macroeconomic analysis, fiscal policy, budget management and intergovernmental fiscal relations. She has published several papers in these areas, including the book entitled *Fiscal Federalism in Theory and Practice*.

Table of contents

CHALLENGES TO FISCAL ADJUSTMENT IN LATIN AMERICA – ISBN 9264022074 © OECD 2006

Box

Tables

Figures

CHALLENGES TO FISCAL ADJUSTMENT IN LATIN AMERICA – ISBN 9264022074 © OECD 2006

Executive summary

This volume discusses fiscal performance and structural reform in the fiscal area in Latin America since the 1990s, with emphasis on Argentina, Brazil, Chile and Mexico. It is based on the proceedings of a seminar on fiscal adjustment in Latin America organised by the Economics Department of the OECD on 10 November 2004 in the context of its work programme with non-member countries in Latin America. These four countries have relatively diverse experiences with fiscal adjustment, which is on-going, underpinning the consolidation of macroeconomic stabilisation in the region, and face a number of common challenges in the years to come.

Assessment and main challenges

Most countries in Latin America have made considerable progress over the years to put their public finances in order. This has been essential for macroeconomic consolidation, and the perception that fiscal discipline is a pre-requisite for sustained, resilient growth appears to be well entrenched in many countries. Underlying fiscal adjustment is a concomitant effort by the more reform-minded governments in the region to strengthen the institutions for macro-fiscal management, reining in sub-national largesse, enhancing transparency and boosting confidence in fiscal policymaking.

But, despite progress in many areas, numerous challenges remain. On expenditure, the overriding challenge is to increase both flexibility in the allocation of budgetary resources, against a backdrop of widespread revenue earmarking in some cases, and the quality of public spending. This also requires dealing pro-actively with the future expenditure pressures associated with the ageing of the population – akin to the OECD experience – and putting in place adequate, cost-effective social safety nets to cushion vulnerable groups against the adverse consequences of macroeconomic volatility, which remains high in the region. Many countries already spend a relatively high share of GDP on social programmes, given their income levels, but social outcomes are often incommensurate with high spending. Efforts to improve the targeting of social programmes, in particular income transfers to vulnerable social groups, and to ensure that the target population has access to services are relatively recent in the region, but are paying off. In any case, careful empirical analysis is, and will

CHALLENGES TO FISCAL ADJUSTMENT IN LATIN AMERICA – ISBN 9264022074 © OECD 2006

continue to be, needed to assess the efficiency of government spending on social programmes, an area where evidence remains predominantly anecdotal.

At the same time, the need for public investment in infrastructure building and upgrading should not be underestimated. Social rates of return are often high in many infrastructure projects in the region due to a still wide "infrastructure deficit" in many areas, justifying government intervention. Many governments are engaging in public-private partnerships (PPP) to finance investment, but will need to guard against the contingent liabilities that might arise due to poor governance and/or the inadequate sharing of risks between the government and its private-sector partners. Moreover, expenditure rigidity, with an increasing weight of statutory and non-discretionary spending in the budget, continues to constrain fiscal adjustment and the ability of governments to respond to changing macroeconomic conditions and to reallocate scarce budgetary resources to finance more meritorious programmes.

On the revenue side, the main challenges are to broaden tax bases, reducing reliance on the more distorting taxes, such as those on financial transactions and enterprise turnover and payroll, and to improve tax administration in many countries. Revenue earmarking and automatic transfers to sub-national levels of government are pervasive in some countries. As a result, when the central government increases its revenue-raising effort in support of fiscal consolidation, part of this revenue is transferred to the sub-national jurisdictions, which are often free to spend it. The experience of Brazil illustrates this phenomenon, where for many years the federal government focused its collection effort on taxes that are not shared with the states and municipalities. The taxation of exports in Argentina is another example of reliance on distorting taxes whose revenue is not shared between the central government and the provinces. In some countries, revenue-to-GDP ratios are too low, reflecting the government's inability to bring more dynamic sectors of the economy into the tax net. As suggested by most of the case studies in this volume, the agenda for reform in the tax area is vast in the region.

On public debt management, the main challenge is for governments to keep indebtedness at a sustainable level, especially where foreign currency-linked instruments account for a large share of the stock of bonded debt. Attention should therefore be focused not only on the size of the public debt in relation to GDP, but also on its structure, including its average maturity, currency composition and indexation mechanisms. A healthy debt structure reduces vulnerabilities, but it is important to recognise that no liability management strategy can succeed if the debt-to-GDP ratio remains high. At the same time, a sustained reduction in public indebtedness is only possible when based on credible policies. Many countries have failed to generate the required primary budget surpluses to offset the impact on the debt dynamics of the recognition of previously unrecorded liabilities, usually as a result of court rulings; the realisation of contingent liabilities, including in the form of support for bank recapitalisation and inadequate risk-sharing with the private sector in PPP projects; or the short-term transition costs of structural measures, including pension reform. These reforms can do much to boost transparency in fiscal operations and to improve the public finances over the longer-term, despite the short-term costs they create for the budget.

The thematic chapters

This volume is divided in two parts. The first deals with cross-country thematic issues, including the role of public indebtedness, the market's perception of fiscal adjustment and the institutional underpinnings of fiscal consolidation. The second is devoted to case studies for the four countries under examination, highlighting successful experiences, areas where further reform is needed and, to the extent possible, comparing and contrasting the Latin American experience with that of OECD countries.

To set the stage, the overview chapter by Luiz de Mello and Nanno Mulder discusses general trends and stylised facts about fiscal adjustment in Latin America since the 1990s, with particular emphasis on Argentina, Brazil, Chile and Mexico. The chapter highlights the considerable diversity in the size and scope of government in these countries, as well as in the level of public indebtedness, which continues to be a source of vulnerability in the higher-debt countries in the region. The authors argue that in most countries the composition of fiscal adjustment has been tilted towards hiking revenue and compressing public investment, rather than retrenching current spending commitments. This imbalance is likely to affect the sustainability of adjustment over time. Moreover, the chapter discusses the scope for using fiscal policy in short-term demand management, arguing that the fiscal stance continues to have a bias towards pro-cyclicality in most cases, reflecting to a large extent high indebtedness and the ensuing vulnerability to shocks in "bad" times, as well as failure to contain the rise in expenditure in "good" times financed by with cyclical revenue windfalls. Failure to smooth the effects of commodity price volatility on the public finances also impedes counter-cyclicality. The chapter concludes by noting that budget and political institutions have a bearing on the government's ability to deliver long-lasting fiscal adjustment, the level of indebtedness it can sustain and the extent of counter-cyclicality it can afford.

The chapter by Lisa Schineller focuses on the market's perception of fiscal adjustment in the region. It reviews the main methodological features of sovereign credit rating and discusses the performance of several Latin American

CHALLENGES TO FISCAL ADJUSTMENT IN LATIN AMERICA – ISBN 9264022074 © OECD 2006

credits. The chapter argues that the sovereign rating methodology is both quantitative and qualitative, reflecting a country's ability and willingness to repay debt on time and in full. It incorporates an assessment of political/institutional credibility and the transparency and predictability of policy by the current and future administrations. In this respect, the author argues that the level of government debt *per se* does not "determine" a rating, which is affected by political and institutional strengths, the fiscal authorities' ability and willingness to adjust policy to shocks or changing economic conditions, the government's policy track record, the structure of public debt (*i.e.* domestic versus foreign currency, maturity), the depth of local capital markets, the sources of external vulnerability, and the economy's growth prospects, among others. In his comments to the chapter, Patrick Lenain focuses on whether credit ratings have contributed to reducing information asymmetry in the case of the Latin American borrowers examined by Lisa Schnieller.

The case studies

The Argentine experience is examined by Pablo Guidotti, who argues against the commonly held view that fiscal management was irresponsible in the 1990s and that the rise in public indebtedness was central to the 2001 crisis. Instead, the author contends that the deterioration of Argentina's public debt dynamics was due to the implementation of pension reform in the early 1990s, the costs to the budget of refinancing at market rates the debt that had been restructured at concessionary rates under the Brady deal of 1992, and the recognition of previously unrecorded liabilities (fiscal "skeletons"). Instead of being perceived by the markets as instrumental in improving Argentina's fiscal accounts over the long term, despite its associated short-term costs, the chapter argues that pension reform contributed to the deterioration of investors' perception of debt sustainability in an environment of macroeconomic volatility and financial crises in other emerging market economies. In his comments to the chapter, Oscar Cetrángolo emphasises the need for further pension reform, including the introduction of a social safety net for the elderly, given the low coverage of Argentina's "second-pillar" fully-funded regime, a phenomenon that is pervasive in several Latin American countries that have engaged in similar pension reforms.

When reviewing the experience of Brazil, the chapter by Fabio Giambiagi and Marcio Ronci examines the country's public-sector accounts since the mid-1990s and argues that the authorities' growing awareness of the need for fiscal discipline was as important as the pace of structural reforms implemented in the period for understanding the dynamics of public indebtedness. Fiscal adjustment intensified after the floating of the *real* in 1999, in an effort to make fiscal policy consistent with the new exchange-rate regime. The chapter discusses the composition of fiscal adjustment, based predominantly on hiking revenue, against the backdrop of Brazil's already high tax-to-GDP ratio, and concludes that fiscal austerity will need to be entrenched in fiscal institutions to make hard-won fiscal discipline sustainable over the longer term. In his comments to the chapter, Juan Carlos Lerda suggests that pressure for higher spending, especially in the social area, is likely to constrain the government's ability to sustain over the longer term the high primary budget surpluses needed to reduce Brazil's debt-to-GDP ratio.

Chile's experience is reviewed by Jose Pablo Arellano, who discusses the driving forces behind the move from chronic budget deficits to structural surpluses and low public indebtedness. The author argues that structural reform since the return to democracy in 1990 has been facilitated by a high degree of political cohesiveness. A key element behind Chile's track record in fiscal rectitude has been the progressive concentration of policymaking powers in the fiscal area on the executive branch of government. The extent of central government control over sub-national finances is in sharp contrast with the other countries examined in this volume. The ban on revenue earmarking is highlighted as a means of rendering fiscal management more flexible. The author posits that the use of fiscal policy as a demand management instrument is due to the introduction of mechanisms to deal with the impact on the budget of fluctuations in copper prices and in the business cycle, an achievement that owes much to Chile's low level of public indebtedness. Financial market scrutiny, an independent central bank and reliance on independent expert panels to set the key parameters to be used in the application of the fiscal rule and the copper price stabilisation mechanism have enhanced transparency and discipline in fiscal policymaking. In his comments to the chapter, Joaquim Oliveira Martins discusses the policy complementarities, particularly in the social and fiscal areas, that may contribute to enhancing Chile's growth potential.

The Mexican experience is analysed by Rogelio Arellano and Fausto Hernández. During the 1970s and early 1980s, persistent budget deficits left the economy ill-prepared to implement the macroeconomic adjustment required in the aftermath of the 1982 debt moratorium. Since then, the authorities have worked towards achieving and sustaining fiscal discipline, including after the 1994-95 Tequila crisis. The chapter discusses different scenarios for Mexico's debt dynamics, arguing that the country has been relatively successful at containing expenditure pressures, while facing important challenges. These include the need to ensure fiscal sustainability over the longer term, given the existence of remaining unrecorded contingent liabilities associated with the public enterprises and the pension system, and to boost revenue performance, against a backdrop of continued reliance on oil revenue.

CHALLENGES TO FISCAL ADJUSTMENT IN LATIN AMERICA – ISBN 9264022074 © OECD 2006

The chapter also discusses the microeconomic aspects of fiscal adjustment, focusing on the need for improving the cost-effectiveness of government spending on infrastructure and social programmes. In her comments to the chapter, Bénédicte Larre argues that it would be interesting to measure the real effort at fiscal consolidation made by the successive administrations through discretionary action, a task that would require the calculation of structural fiscal indicators as those available at the OECD for a number of its Member countries.

Panel discussions

In recognition of the political-economy dimensions of fiscal adjustment, a panel discussion followed the presentation of the case studies. The panellists were asked to discuss their experiences in policymaking in periods of fiscal adjustment. The panel was chaired by Val Koromzay and included José Pablo Arellano, Mario Blejer, Jorge Braga de Macedo, Pablo Guidotti and Teresa Ter-Minassian, whose experience as a senior negotiator and overseer of several IMF-supported programmes in the region offered a complementary perspective on the political economy of reform to that of the other panellists.

Various panellists stressed the fragilities that remain in fiscal adjustment in the region, as well as noting that public opinion support for reform has waned in several countries in recent years. While acknowledging that fiscal adjustment has been impressive in some countries, in the sense of delivering a move from chronic budget deficits to sizeable surpluses in a relatively short time span, the panellists noted that the main weakness of fiscal adjustment in the region has been the reliance on cuts in public investment and, in some cases, social safety nets, which are difficult to sustain over time. Revenue-raising measures have often focused on distorting taxes, such as those on financial transactions and enterprise turnover. Public opinion support has faltered, encouraging the adoption of populist measures in some cases, because the reforms' pay-off in terms of higher, more resilient growth and an improvement in the quality of public services and living standards, has not always materialised as swiftly as expected.

Panellists were of the view that several conditions need to be fulfilled for fiscal adjustment to be sustainable. These include:

- The process of discussing, approving and implementing structural reform is very important, an area where the legislature has a key role to play. To this end, policymakers should create constituencies in support of reform, which can be achieved by adequately compensating those who are likely to be affected most adversely by the reforms, including through the introduction of social safety nets, as well as communicating effectively to society at large and other stakeholders the benefits of reform.

- Although budget institutions are deeply rooted in history and legal traditions, control over the budget process should preferably be concentrated in few stakeholders who have strong incentives to commit themselves to fiscal discipline.

- The timing of reform also affects its likelihood of success. While financial stress highlights the urgency of reform, it may also make fiscal consolidation less likely to be sustainable, including by encouraging a focus on short-term, one-off measures which may not be conducive to fiscal discipline over the longer term.

- The maintenance of fiscal discipline requires sound institutions, which can make fiscal policymaking predictable and transparent. The introduction of fiscal rules, with the enactment of "Fiscal Responsibility" legislation in many countries, is not a sufficient condition for the strengthening of institutions, unless the law is respected both in letter and spirit. A constructive relationship between the executive branch of government and the legislature and the judiciary is also important to make the process of institutional reform more co-operative and therefore less prone to capture by interest groups.

CHALLENGES TO FISCAL ADJUSTMENT IN LATIN AMERICA – ISBN 9264022074 © OECD 2006

Chapter 1

Fiscal adjustment in Latin America: Trends and stylised facts

Luiz de Mello and Nanno Mulder,

OECD Economics Department

This chapter presents general trends and stylised facts about fiscal adjustment in Latin America since the 1990s, with particular emphasis on Argentina, Brazil, Chile and Mexico. It highlights the considerable diversity in the size and scope of government among these countries, as well as in the level of public indebtedness, which continues to be a source of vulnerability in the higher-debt countries in the region. In most countries, the composition of fiscal adjustment has been tilted towards hiking revenue and compressing public investment, rather than retrenching current spending commitments. This imbalance is likely to affect the sustainability of adjustment over time. Moreover, the fiscal stance continues to have a bias towards pro-cyclicality in most cases, reflecting to a large extent high indebtedness and the ensuing vulnerability to shocks in "bad" times, as well as failure to contain the rise in expenditure in "good" times financed by cyclical revenue windfalls.

Introduction

Since the early 1990s, many countries in Latin America have made substantial progress in consolidating their public finances, but important differences remain across countries with regard to fiscal performance. Following a long period of fiscal disarray, which resulted in chronic inflation, especially during most of the 1980s, budget deficits were trimmed, reliance on inflation-tax revenue was reduced and the real value of public debt was no longer eroded by inflation. Many countries recognised contingent and off-budget liabilities as an integral part of fiscal adjustment and as a means of boosting transparency in fiscal policymaking. As a result, the fiscal policy stance has become more reactive to changes in indebtedness and some countries have worked towards making fiscal consolidation more permanent by improving public expenditure management and control, as well as upgrading budget institutions.

Notwithstanding area-wide progress in fiscal consolidation, fiscal performance has differed across countries. This chapter will compare and contrast trends and highlight stylised facts in fiscal adjustment in Latin America since the early 1990s, with particular emphasis on Argentina, Brazil, Chile and Mexico. These four countries have relatively diverse experiences with fiscal adjustment, facing some common challenges in the years to come.

The main issues to be highlighted are as follows:

- There is considerable diversity in the size and scope of government among Latin American countries. Governments are typically much smaller in Latin America than in the OECD area and the composition of government expenditure and revenue varies considerably across countries.

- Public debt levels also differ significantly across countries in Latin America, being a considerable source of vulnerability in the higher-debt countries. Policy effort towards fiscal adjustment is on-going in the reforming countries, underpinning the consolidation of macroeconomic stabilisation in the region.

- In most countries in Latin America, the composition of fiscal adjustment has been tilted towards hiking revenue and compressing public investment, rather than retrenching current spending. This is likely to affect the sustainability of adjustment over time.

CHALLENGES TO FISCAL ADJUSTMENT IN LATIN AMERICA – ISBN 9264022074 © OECD 2006

- The fiscal stance continues to have a bias towards pro-cyclicality in most cases, reflecting to a large extent high indebtedness and the ensuing vulnerability to external shocks in "bad" times, as well as failure to contain the rise in expenditure in "good" times on the back of cyclical, often commodity price-related, revenue windfalls.

- Budget and political institutions have a bearing on the government's ability to deliver long-lasting fiscal adjustment, the level of indebtedness it can sustain, and the extent of counter-cyclicality it can afford.

The size and scope of government

Governments are typically much smaller in Latin America than in the OECD area. Measuring the size of government using ratios of expenditure and revenue to GDP is affected by the coverage of the fiscal accounts, which varies a great deal in the region (Box 1.1). Expenditure-to-GDP ratios for the consolidated central government – based on information available from the IMF's *Government Financial Statistics* – suggests that the government is of similar sizes in Argentina, Chile and Mexico, but much larger in Brazil (Figure 1.1). Data available from national sources for the public sector as a whole (including lower tiers of government and the non-financial public enterprise sector), although not readily comparable across countries, suggests that the government is much larger in Argentina and Brazil, predominantly on account of sizeable sub-national jurisdictions, than in Chile or Mexico.

Box 1.1. **The coverage of fiscal accounts in Argentina, Brazil, Chile and Mexico**

The coverage of the fiscal accounts varies considerably, making cross-country comparisons difficult. Whereas OECD fiscal data are largely comparable across countries, this is much less the case for Latin America at large. Recent initiatives to standardise fiscal statistics include that of the MERCOSUR countries through the Macroeconomic Monitoring Group (GMM), which now produces comparable statistics for the budget balances (headline and primary) and public indebtedness for the full and associated member countries.

For the purpose of this chapter, data on government revenue and expenditure are available from the IMF's *Government Finance Statistics* for the consolidated central government and from national sources (see below). Data on public indebtedness and budget balances (overall and primary) are available from national sources.

Box 1.1. **The coverage of fiscal accounts in Argentina, Brazil, Chile and Mexico**
(*cont'd*)

The coverage of the fiscal statistics readily available from national sources is as follows:

- **Argentina**. The "national non-financial public sector" refers to the central government and the social security system, thereby excluding the provinces and the non-financial public enterprises. Data are available from the Budget Office (*Secretaría de Hacienda*).

- **Brazil**. The consolidated public sector comprises the central government (federal government, social security system and the central bank), the regional governments (states and municipalities) and the non-financial public enterprises (all levels of government). Data on budget outturns refer to the public sector financing requirement (PSBR). Data are available from the Central Bank of Brazil and the National Treasury (*Secretaria do Tesouro Nacional*).

- **Chile**. The general government comprises the budgetary central government and the municipalities, thereby excluding the public enterprises and the central bank. Data are available from the Budget Office (*Dirección de Presupuestos*).

- **Mexico**. The public sector comprises the federal government and the non-financial public enterprises under budgetary control. Budget outturn data refer to the financial balance, although the public sector financing requirement (PSBR) is also available. Data are available from the budget Office (*Secretaría de Hacienda y Crédito Público*).

The composition of revenue and expenditure differs across countries and in comparison with the OECD area.[1] Based on the functional composition of expenditure, Argentina and Brazil spend proportionally more on social protection and general public services than Chile and Mexico, reflecting differences in the scope of government within the region. Latin American countries also differ in terms of flexibility in the allocation of public funds. In Argentina and Brazil, for example, mandated spending (*i.e.* constitutionally-mandated spending floors and transfers to lower levels of government) accounts for 60 and 80% of total primary spending, respectively.[2] Turning to the composition of revenue, direct taxes account for a larger share of revenue in the OECD area than in Latin America, possibly reflecting widespread informality in the region. The share of social security contributions is comparable in Brazil to the OECD average, whereas it is very low in Chile, owing essentially to the privatisation of the pension system in the early 1980s. Property taxes continue to carry a small weight in central government revenue in the region, except for Brazil.

Figure 1.1. **Size and scope of government, 1990-97**
In per cent of GDP, consolidated central government

A. Size of government (expenditure-to-GDP ratios)

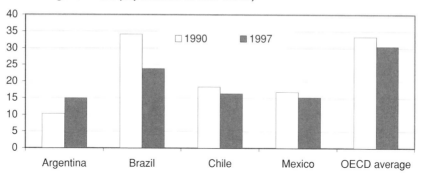

B. Composition of expenditure: Functional classification, 1997

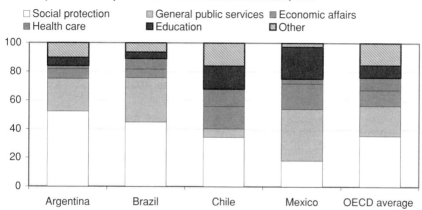

C. Composition of revenue, 1997

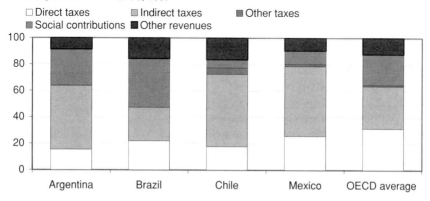

Source: *Government Financial Statistics*, IMF.

The sustainability of public indebtedness

As a general trend, public debt ratios fell in Latin America as a whole during 1990-97 and increased between 1998-2003, except for Chile and Mexico (Figure 1.2). The slowdown in economic growth in the second half of the 1990s contributed to the upward trend in public debt ratios in Argentina and Brazil. Gradual disinflation in most countries reduced their reliance on inflation-tax revenue and the erosion of the real value of debt. Public indebtedness has also been affected by balance-sheet adjustments, reflecting the recognition of contingent and off-balance sheet liabilities in many countries, as well as those associated with bank restructuring. Moreover, the collapse of exchange rate pegs contributed to the revaluation of foreign currency-indexed/denominated liabilities, also increasing public debt ratios. This was the case, for example, in Argentina (2001), Brazil (1999) and Mexico (1995).

High indebtedness is an important source of vulnerability in the region. Debt levels that are considered sustainable tend to be lower in emerging market economies in general than in their more mature counterparts. The ability of emerging market economies to repay and re-finance outstanding debt

Figure 1.2. **Public indebtedness, 1990-2003**
In per cent of GDP

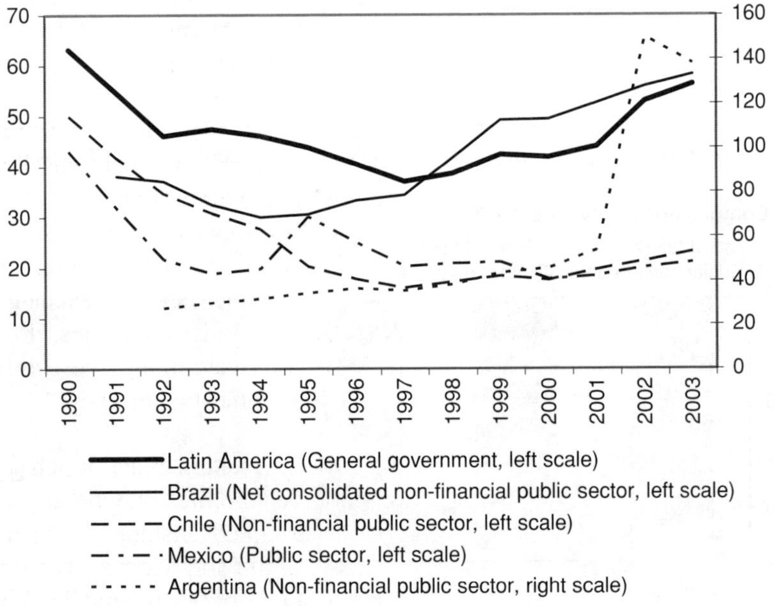

Latin America (General government, left scale)
Brazil (Net consolidated non-financial public sector, left scale)
Chile (Non-financial public sector, left scale)
Mexico (Public sector, left scale)
Argentina (Non-financial public sector, right scale)

Source: ECLAC.

CHALLENGES TO FISCAL ADJUSTMENT IN LATIN AMERICA – ISBN 9264022074 © OECD 2006

obligations is curtailed by their lower revenue ratios, more volatile tax bases and higher, more volatile spending on debt service. Budget financing is also affected by supply-side constraints, given imperfect access to international capital markets and shallow domestic financial markets. Many emerging market economies also face "debt intolerance", in the sense that credit ratings often differ for the same level of indebtedness, reflecting individual countries' track record in external debt repayment and macroeconomic stability.[3] Against this background, a number of analysts suggest that debt levels above 30-50% of GDP may not be sustainable in Latin America.[4] Most OECD countries can sustain higher debt levels but should be concerned about public indebtedness because of the need to prepare for the ageing of the population and to pursue macroeconomic efficiency, as high indebtedness requires higher taxes and puts upward pressure on real interest rates, crowding out private investment.

Not only the level, but also the composition, of debt matter. Vulnerability is heightened by the prevalence in domestic public debt of securities paying floating interest rates and/or indexed to the exchange rate or denominated in foreign currency, which has nevertheless been reduced over time in most countries, coupled with relatively short maturities (Table 1.1).[5] In the case of Brazil, for example, foreign exchange-indexed securities (including foreign exchange swaps) accounted for about 40% of the securitized public debt stock in the run-up to the presidential election of October 2002, a period marked by considerable financial duress. As a result, a 10% depreciation of the exchange rate was associated with an increase in the net debt ratio by 3.2 percentage points. This elasticity has come down considerably since then as a result of the gradual retirement of exchange rate-indexed securities as financial conditions have improved. In Mexico, the share of exchange rate-denominated debt peaked prior to the *peso* collapse in December 1994. Concern over debt sustainability makes budget financing sensitive to changes in market sentiment, which is exacerbated by the region's long history of debt crises, sovereign debt defaults and the recourse to inflationary financing of the domestic debt (an implicit form of default). The relatively high exposure of public debt to exchange rate volatility in Chile is compensated by relatively long maturities. Recently, Brazil, Chile and Mexico have shown signs of overcoming the original-sin problem by issuing bonds abroad denominated in domestic currency.

Debt sustainability depends on how policymakers react to changes in indebtedness. Governments in emerging market economies may be less willing, or unable, to respond promptly and in a sustained fashion to changes in indebtedness. In the case of Argentina, Brazil, Chile and Mexico, governments have reacted, albeit to different extents, to high or rising indebtedness by delivering higher primary surpluses so as to ensure the sustainability of the debt

Table 1.1. **Public debt indicators**
In per cent

	Argen-tina	Brazil		Chile		Mexico	
	2004	1999	2004	2000	2004	1994	2004
Composition of securitised public debt stock by index (in per cent)							
Fixed-rate securities	..	9.0	20.1	..	..	23.0	62.0
Floating-rate securities	..	57.0	52.4	..	..	4.9	29.9
Exchange rate-indexed securities[2]	88.3	22.8	9.9	87.7	71.2	54.6	0.0
Inflation-indexed securities	..	5.6	14.9	12.3	28.8	17.4	8.1
Other	11.7	5.6	2.7	0.0	0.0	0.0	0.0
Average maturity of debt stock (in years)[3]	7.8	2.3	2.3	13.3	11.2	1.5	2.9
Short-term debt[4] (in per cent of debt total)	39.9	54.9	46.1	..	1.9	..	..
Memorandum items:							
Floating-rate debt (in per cent of public sector net debt)	30.5	..	..	90.0	73.8	..	..
Defaulted debt and central bank loans (in per cent of total debt)	26.0	..	..	..	..	..	..

1. Debt statistics refer to the federal domestic publicly traded debt in Brazil, the total public sector debt in Argentina and Chile, and the federal securitised debt in Mexico.
2. Includes foreign exchange swaps in Brazil and excludes defaulted debt and central bank loans in Argentina.
3. Excludes defaulted capital and interest payments in Argentina.
4. Refers to debt falling due in less than 12 months. Includes defaulted debt and central bank loans in Argentina.
Source: *Secretaría de Hacienda*, Argentina; *Secretaria do Tesouro Nacional*, Brazil; *Dirección de Presupuestos*, Chile; *Secretaría de Hacienda y Crédito Público*, Mexico.

dynamics over time (Figure 1.3).[6] These co-movements, which provide only *prima facie* evidence of a strong reaction of fiscal stance to indebtedness, appear to be more strongly correlated the higher the level of indebtedness and the faster the pace of increase in the debt-to-GDP ratio. However, policy reactivity tends to be stronger in more mature economies. Recent research suggests that primary balances tend to have lower sensitivity to indebtedness in emerging market economies than in industrial countries, controlling for other determinants of fiscal stance. This sensitivity is also affected by the level of indebtedness: it is estimated to be lower in emerging markets as the debt-to-GDP ratio rises (and not statistically significant when debt exceeds 50% of GDP) than in industrial countries.[7] Episodes of sizeable corrective action in the face of high or rising indebtedness are not uncommon in the OECD area.[8]

CHALLENGES TO FISCAL ADJUSTMENT IN LATIN AMERICA – ISBN 9264022074 © OECD 2006

Figure 1.3. **Indebtedness and fiscal stance, 1990-2003**
In per cent of GDP

——————— Public debt
(at time t, right axis)

- - - - - - - Primary budget balance
(at time t+1, left axis)

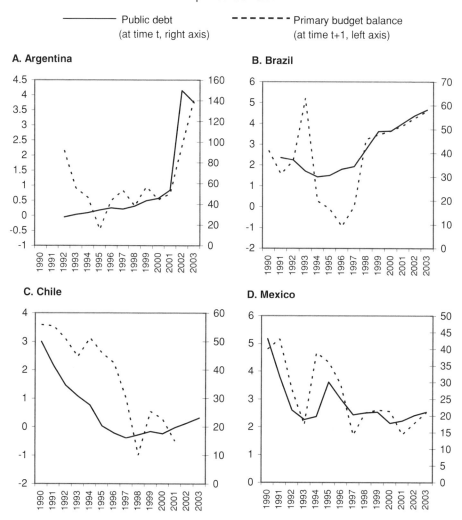

A. Argentina

B. Brazil

C. Chile

D. Mexico

Source: *Secretaría de Hacienda*, Argentina; *Secretaria do Tesouro Nacional*, Brazil; *Dirección de Presupuestos*, Chile; *Secretaría de Hacienda y Crédito Público*, Mexico.

Trends in fiscal adjustment

There are considerable differences in the magnitude and timing of fiscal adjustment in Latin America. As a general trend, budget outturns, measured by the headline budget balance (unadjusted for the business cycle), improved in the

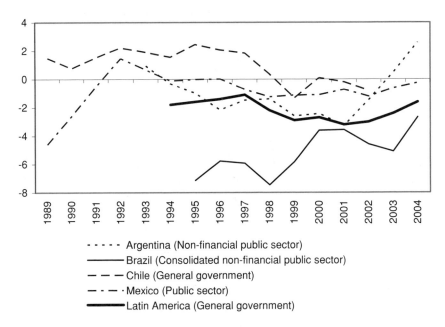

Figure 1.4. **Budget outcomes, 1989-2003**
Headline budget balance in per cent of GDP

- - - - - Argentina (Non-financial public sector)
————— Brazil (Consolidated non-financial public sector)
— — — Chile (General government)
— · — · Mexico (Public sector)
▬▬▬▬ Latin America (General government)

Source: *Secretaría de Hacienda*, Argentina; *Secretaria do Tesouro Nacional*, Brazil; *Dirección de Presupuestos*, Chile; *Secretaría de Hacienda y Crédito Público*, Mexico.

mid-1990s until 1997 and then again after 2001 (Figure 1.4). Area-wide trends need to be interpreted with caution because they are affected by differences in the coverage of fiscal accounts across countries. In any case, fiscal adjustment has taken place against a background of volatile growth, continued disinflation and strengthening external positions, facilitated by improvements in the terms of trade in some cases (Figure 1.5). Debt service payments also affected the budget balances, in particular in Brazil.

The composition of fiscal adjustment has also differed across countries. While efforts have been made to broaden the tax base and combat tax evasion, against the backdrop of relatively low ratios of revenue to GDP, with the exception of Brazil, downward rigidity in spending has resulted in a compression of capital outlays (Figure 1.6), as well as social spending (except social security benefits) in some countries.[9] A case in point is the earmarking of revenue, which is widespread, and the introduction of spending floors for selected social programmes in Brazil over the years, as well as mandated revenue sharing with sub-national levels of government, as illustrated by the Argentine experience.[10] The composition of adjustment is known to affect its likelihood of success in the sense of delivering a sustained reduction in indebtedness. Empirical evidence for the OECD countries suggests that fiscal adjustment is more successful when based on the retrenchment of current expenditure, rather than on hiking revenue and/or cutting back public investment.[11]

Figure 1.5. **Macroeconomic indicators, 1994-2003**

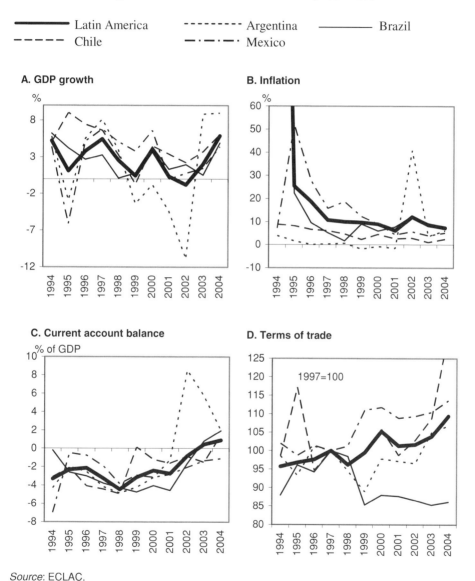

Source: ECLAC.

Figure 1.6. **Composition of fiscal adjustment**[1]
In per cent of GDP

A. Argentina: Total revenue and primary expenditure

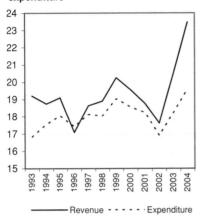

Revenue ----- Expenditure

B. Argentina: Selected revenue and expenditure items

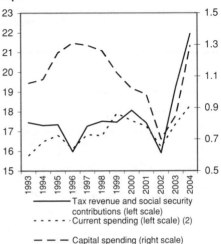

———— Tax revenue and social security contributions (left scale)
----- Current spending (left scale) (2)
— — Capital spending (right scale)

C. Brazil: Total revenue and primary expenditure

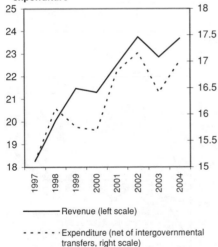

———— Revenue (left scale)
----- Expenditure (net of intergovernmental transfers, right scale)

D. Brazil: Selected revenue and expenditure items

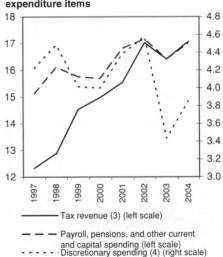

———— Tax revenue (3) (left scale)
— — Payroll, pensions, and other current and capital spending (left scale)
----- Discretionary spending (4) (right scale)

1. Refers to the non-financial public sector in Argentina, the central government in Brazil and Mexico, and the general government in Chile.
2. Refers to payroll, social security benefits, transfers to provinces and other current spending.
3. Includes revenue from federal "contributions".
4. Measured as "other OCCs".
Source: *Secretaría de Hacienda*, Argentina; *Secretaria do Tesouro Nacional*, Brazil; *Dirección de Presupuestos*, Chile; *Secretaría de Hacienda y Crédito Público*, Mexico

CHALLENGES TO FISCAL ADJUSTMENT IN LATIN AMERICA – ISBN 9264022074 © OECD 2006

Figure 1.6. **Composition of fiscal adjustment** (*cont'd*)
In per cent of GDP

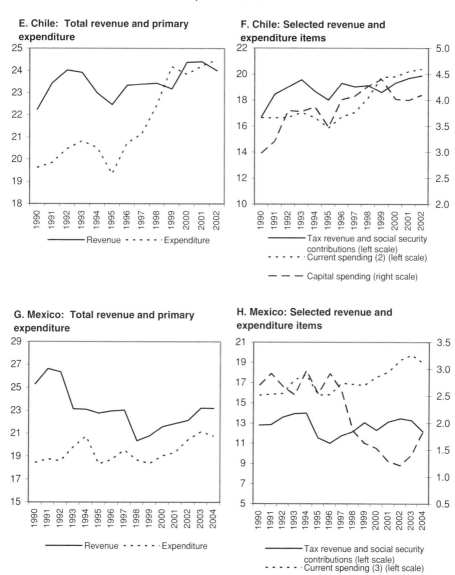

E. Chile: Total revenue and primary expenditure

Revenue ——— Expenditure ‑ ‑ ‑ ‑ ‑

F. Chile: Selected revenue and expenditure items

Tax revenue and social security contributions (left scale) ———
Current spending (2) (left scale) ‑ ‑ ‑ ‑ ‑
Capital spending (right scale) — — —

G. Mexico: Total revenue and primary expenditure

Revenue ——— Expenditure ‑ ‑ ‑ ‑ ‑

H. Mexico: Selected revenue and expenditure items

Tax revenue and social security contributions (left scale) ———
Current spending (3) (left scale) ‑ ‑ ‑ ‑ ‑
Capital spending (right scale) — — —

1. Refers to the non-financial public sector in Argentina, the central government in Brazil and Mexico, and the general government in Chile.
2. Refers to payroll, social security benefits, transfers to provinces and other current spending.
3. Includes revenue from federal "contributions".
4. Measured as "other OCCs".

Source: *Secretaría de Hacienda*, Argentina; *Secretaria do Tesouro Nacional*, Brazil; *Dirección de Presupuestos*, Chile; *Secretaría de Hacienda y Crédito Público*, Mexico.

Fiscal stance over the cycle

The responsiveness of the fiscal stance to the business cycle reflects differences in the size of automatic stabilisers across countries, which tend to be larger in the OECD area than in Latin America.[12] In the OECD area, the fiscal stance tends to be predominantly counter-cyclical in bad times, but episodes of discretionary pro-cyclical easing are not uncommon in upturns.[13] Evidence for the OECD countries suggests that high tax ratios allow for greater automatic stabilisation, but tax cuts implemented during upturns often reduce the scope for counter-cyclical easing in subsequent downturns. Also, fiscal tightening during downturns is somewhat less likely to occur in the presence of expenditure rigidities. This is the case when, for example, payroll outlays, which are harder to retrench than capital spending, account for a large share of government spending and when the government is a sizeable employer relative to the private sector. This is likely to be the case in Latin America, but empirical evidence is not readily available. Greater pro-cyclicality in Latin America relative to the OECD countries is also related to the higher volatility of the tax base in the former region.[14]

High public indebtedness contributes to pro-cyclicality.[15] Concern about the sustainability of public indebtedness, which is high in Latin America, calls for corrective action even in periods of below-potential growth (Figure 1.7). This makes fiscal consolidation, rather than short-term demand management, the overriding objective of fiscal policymaking in the more indebted countries.[16] Moreover, pro-cyclicality seems to depend on public governance, as during economic upturns voters may not trust the government to accumulate assets or reserves, and may urge it instead to cut taxes.[17]

International liquidity conditions, affecting investors' appetite for risky assets, are likely to deteriorate in downturns, when domestic financing costs tend to rise, making pro-cyclicality in Latin America typically more severe in downturns.[18] Relatively low ratios of foreign trade to GDP also reduce the region's capacity to absorb external financial shocks. The OECD experience suggests that public indebtedness is a key determinant of whether fiscal stance is pro-cyclical during downturns. But it is important to note that fiscal consolidation in bad times need not be destabilising so long as it restores confidence by putting the debt dynamics on a sustainable path.[19] In Chile and Mexico, the steady reduction in the public debt ratio over time has provided more room for manoeuvre, making fiscal stance more counter-cyclical.

The fiscal stance is sensitive to terms-of-trade shocks in Latin America. This is because the tax base tends to be more volatile in commodity-exporting countries and, as a result, failure to stabilise commodity price-related revenue

CHALLENGES TO FISCAL ADJUSTMENT IN LATIN AMERICA – ISBN 9264022074 © OECD 2006

often results in pro-cyclicality (Figure 1.8). When tax bases are volatile, full tax smoothing would require large budget surpluses in good times and large budget deficits in bad times, which may be difficult to finance. Against this

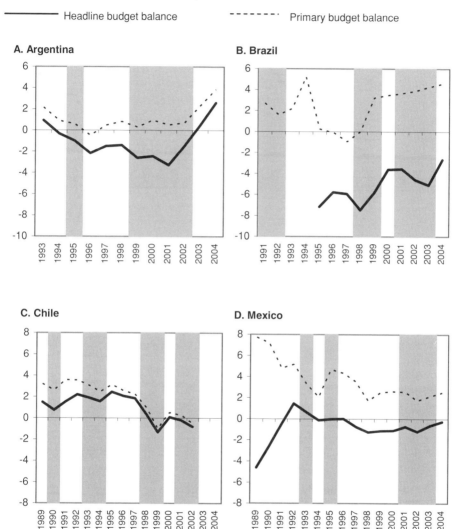

Figure 1.7. **Fiscal stance over the business cycle**[1]
In per cent of GDP

1. The grey areas identify cyclical downturns, defined as the years in which changes in the output gap relative to the previous year are non-positive. The output gap is calculated as the per cent difference between actual and HP-filtered GDP.

Source: *Secretaría de Hacienda*, Argentina; *Secretaria do Tesouro Nacional*, Brazil; *Dirección de Presupuestos*, Chile; *Secretaría de Hacienda y Crédito Público*, Mexico.

Figure 1.8. **Fiscal stance over the terms-of-trade cycle**[1]
In per cent of GDP

——————— Headline budget balance   -------- Primary budget balance

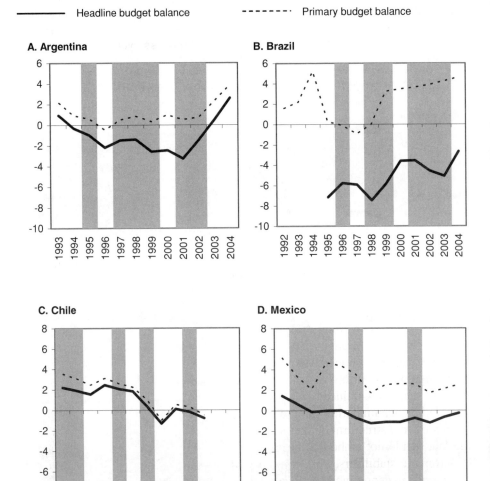

A. Argentina

B. Brazil

C. Chile

D. Mexico

1.   The grey areas identify cyclical downturns, defined as the years in which changes
in the terms of trade relative to the previous year are non-positive and less that
3 per cent in magnitude.
Source: *Secretaría de Hacienda*, Argentina; *Secretaria do Tesouro Nacional*, Brazil; *Dirección de Presupuestos*, Chile; *Secretaría de Hacienda y Crédito Público*, Mexico.

background, the creation of stabilisation funds is an appropriate mechanism for insulating fiscal policy from terms-of-trade cycles in commodity-exporting countries, ensuring the accumulation of resources during booms and the

CHALLENGES TO FISCAL ADJUSTMENT IN LATIN AMERICA – ISBN 9264022074 © OECD 2006

withdrawal of assets during cyclical downturns. The experience of such funds in Chile (copper) and Mexico (oil) are a case in point.[20] In any event, the successful functioning of stabilisation funds requires setting a reference price for the relevant commodity in budget formulation based on conservative medium-run projections, as well as transparent operating rules for using fund resources according to fluctuations in commodity prices.

The role of institutions

Budget institutions affect the sustainability of fiscal adjustment and the responsiveness of the fiscal stance to the business cycle. Several countries have adopted "Fiscal Responsibility" legislation in support of fiscal consolidation, enhancing their ability to control expenditure. The scope of legislation varies across countries, as well as its coverage. Fiscal rules preventing the central bank and public financial institutions from lending to the government and disciplining sub-national finances have been instrumental in fiscal consolidation in the region. Brazil's legislation is particularly noteworthy, given the extension of legal provisions to all levels of government.[21] Prudential regulations limiting banks' exposure to government debt, including that of sub-national levels of government, is also important.

Certain types of fiscal rule, particularly those requiring actual, rather than cyclically-adjusted, budgets to be in balance, automatically damp cyclical fluctuations in the budget balance. Evidence for the United States, where the states have had a variety of balanced-budget rules for a relatively long period, suggests that rules-induced pro-cyclicality cannot be ruled out, but it can be mitigated by accumulating rainy day funds in good times.[22] Chile's commitment since 2001 to a structural budget surplus of 1% of GDP is an example of a fiscal rule that, while not embodied in law, enhances the ability of the government to let automatic stabilisers work to some extent and symmetrically in reaction to fluctuations in economic growth and terms of trade.

Institutions affect the level of indebtedness countries can sustain. Budget institutions that are hierarchical, transparent and aimed at strengthening expenditure control affect the level of the primary surplus that can be generated and maintained for a sustained period of time, contributing to boosting the government's reactivity to changes in indebtedness.[23] But political, not only budget, institutions also affect the responsiveness of the fiscal stance to the business cycle. Evidence for Latin America suggests that countries with a large degree of proportionality (large districts and high political fragmentation) in their electoral systems often have larger governments, larger deficits and more pro-cyclical fiscal policy.[24] This is also the case, by and large, in the OECD area, where undesirable pro-cyclical retrenchment seems less prevalent in countries with more politically fragmented governments and electoral systems based on proportional representation, rather than plurality (*i.e.* first-past-the-post regimes). Electoral cycles have a role to play and pro-cyclical retrenchment appears to be less common in election years.

Notes

1.   See Stein, Talvi and Grisanti (1999) and Martner and Tromben (2004a) for more information on trends in revenue and expenditure composition in Latin America.

2.   See IMF (2005) for more information.

3.   Reinhart *et al.* (2003) show that external debt intolerance is a good predictor of domestic debt default.

4.   See, for example, Martner and Tromben (2004b), IMF (2003, 2005) and Singh *et al.* (2005). IMF (2003) shows that the maximum ratio of sustainable public debt to GDP for emerging market economies is substantially lower than that for industrial economies. The ability of governments to adjust primary spending to changing indebtedness conditions is also taken into account. Mendoza and Oviedo (2004) show that the public debt ratios of Brazil and Colombia were above the estimated tolerable maximum during 1996-2002.

5.   The preponderance of dollar-denominated or indexed securities arises from the difficulty of emerging market economies to borrow in their own currency ("original sin"). Borrowing in a foreign currency creates a currency mismatch in a country's balance sheet and is associated with larger output and capital-flow volatility, lower credit ratings and more rigid monetary policies. In the period 1999-2001, out of US$ 1.3 trillion of debt issued by international organisations and countries other than those holding the 5 major currencies (British Pound, Euro, Swiss Franc, US dollar and Yen), only 15% was issued in domestic currency (Eichengreen, Hausmann, and Panizza, 2002).

6.   See de Mello (2005) for empirical evidence on debt sustainability in Brazil.

7.   See IMF (2003), Chapter III, for more information.

CHALLENGES TO FISCAL ADJUSTMENT IN LATIN AMERICA – ISBN 9264022074 © OECD 2006

8.   See de Mello, Kongsrud and Price (2004) for more information.

9.   More than one-half of total fiscal adjustment in Argentina, Bolivia, Brazil, Chile and Peru during the 1990s was accounted for by a reduction in infrastructure investment (Calderón, Easterly and Servén, 2002). Regarding social spending, Wodon *et al.* (2002) found that, for a sample of 7 Latin American countries during the 1980s and 1990s, public social spending per poor person was reduced during recessions by two percentage points for each percentage point decrease in per capita GDP.

10.   For more information on spending rigidities in Brazil see OECD (2005a).

11.   Evidence for Latin America is limited. Evidence for the OECD countries was pioneered by Alesina and Perotti (1997) and suggests that cuts in public investment are not sustainable. Governments that are able to cut the politically more delicate components of the budget (public employment, social security, welfare programmes) may signal that they are more committed to serious fiscal adjustment. McDermott and Wescott (1996) also obtain the same results. Fiscal consolidations based on cuts in the expenditure side, especially transfers and government wages, are more likely to succeed in reducing the debt ratio. Rocha and Picchetti (2003) use Alesina and Perotti's (1997) methodology to show that the fiscal consolidation in 1994 in Brazil was likely to be unsuccessful as it was achieved on the back of public investment retrenchment, while wages and transfers remained unchanged.

12.   See van den Noord (2000) and Lane (2003) for evidence for OECD countries. Using data for 87 countries for the period 1960-99, Alesina and Tabellini (2005) show that Latin America was the region with the most pro-cyclical fiscal stance.

13.   See OECD (2003a), Chapter IV, for more information.

14.   See Talvi and Vegh (2000) for more information.

15.   See ECLAC (2003, 2004) for more information.

16.   According to ECLAC, in 13 out of the 17 cases in which GDP growth was above trend, the change in the cyclically-adjusted public-sector balance was negative, reflecting an expansionary fiscal policy. There are also episodes in which the budget balance adjusted for the business cycle exhibited little variation despite significant changes in the output gap, such as in Chile (1992-98), Brazil (1990-94) and Mexico (1995-97). See Martner and Tromben (2004b) for more information.

17.   See Alesina and Tabellini (2005) for more information.

18.   See Gavin *et al.* (1996) for empirical evidence.

19.   A corrective fiscal contraction may become expansionary in a downturn, and hence counter-cyclical. In this case, the gain in credibility outweighs the negative multiplier effect associated with fiscal contractions, making it expansionary. For example, Giavazzi *et al.* (2000), as well as Alesina and Ardagna (1998), among others, show that fiscal contractions may be expansionary in indebted OECD countries and that the composition of adjustment, via tax increases and/or expenditure cuts, affects the expansionary potential of fiscal retrenchment.

20.   Colombia's coffee fund is another example. See Perry (2003) for more information. See OECD (2004) for an assessment of Mexico's oil fund, and OECD (2003b) for more information on Chile's copper fund.

21.   See IMF (2001) for more information.

22.   Evidence provided by Sorensen *et al.* (2001) suggests that the states that have relatively tight balanced-budget rules seem to have less pronounced swings in both revenue and expenditure over the cycle than the states with less stringent fiscal rules. This is consistent with the evidence reported by Bohn and Inman (1996), which, although sensitive to the cyclical indicator used to gauge fiscal responsiveness, indicates that stringent fiscal rules encourage precautionary savings in good times, which can be used subsequently to finance counter-cyclical measures in bad times. By contrast, also using US state data, Alesina and Bayoumi (1996) argue that fiscal rules have indeed reduced flexibility in state-level fiscal policymaking without, however, having a bearing on the cyclicality of state fiscal policy.

23.   Empirical evidence on Latin America by Alesina *et al.* (1999) shows that the countries with budget procedures allowing legislative constraints on the deficit, and which are hierarchical (*i.e.* strong government relative to legislature) and transparent, had lower primary deficits during 1989-93.

24.   See Stein, Talvi and Grisanti (1999) for more information.

CHALLENGES TO FISCAL ADJUSTMENT IN LATIN AMERICA – ISBN 9264022074 © OECD 2006

Bibliography

Alesina, A. and S. Ardagna (1998), "Tales of Fiscal Contractions", *Economic Policy*, Vol. 27, pp. 489-545.

Alesina, A. and T. Bayoumi (1996), "The Costs and Benefits of Fiscal Rules: Evidence from US States", *NBER Working Paper*, No. 5614, NBER, Cambridge, MA.

Alesina, A. and R. Perotti (1997). "Fiscal Adjustments in OECD Countries: Composition and Macroeconomic Effects", *IMF Staff Papers*, Vol. 44, No. 2, pp. 210–48.

Alesina, A., R. Hausmann, R. Hommes and E. Stein (1999), "Budget Institutions and Fiscal Performance in Latin America", *Journal of Development Economics*, Vol. 59, No. 2, pp. 253-73.

Alberto, A. and G. Tabellini (2005), "Why is Fiscal Policy Often Procyclical?, Unpublished document, Harvard and Bocconi University.

Bohn, H. and R.P. Inman (1996), "Balanced-Budget Rules and Public Deficits: Evidence from the U.S. States", *Carnegie-Rochester Conference Series on Public Policy,* Vol. 45, pp. 13-76.

Calderón, C., W. Easterly and L. Servén (2002), "Infrastructure Compression and Public Sector Solvency in Latin America", *Working Paper*, No. 187, Central Bank of Chile, Santiago.

de Mello, L., P.M. Kongsrud and R. Price (2004), "Fiscal Stance over the Cycle", *Economics Department Working Paper*, No. 397, OECD, Paris.

de Mello, L. (2005), "Estimating a Fiscal Reaction Function: The Case of Debt Sustainability in Brazil", *Applied Economics*, forthcoming.

ECLAC (2003), *Balance Preliminar de las Economias de America Latina y el Caribe*, ECLAC, Santiago.

ECLAC (2004, 2005), *Estudio Económico de América Latina y el Caribe*, ECLAC, Santiago.

Eichengreen, B., R. Hausmann and U. Panizza (2002), "Original Sin: The Pain, the Mystery, and the Road to Redemption", Paper presented at the Conference on Currency and Maturity Mismatching: Redeeming Debt from Original Sin", 21-22 November", Inter-American Development Bank, Washington, D.C.

Gavin, M., R. Hausmann, R. Perotti and E. Talvi (1996), "Managing Fiscal Policy in Latin America and the Caribbean: Volatility, Procyclicality, and Limited Creditworthiness", *Working Paper*, No. 326, Inter-American Development Bank, Washington, D.C.

Giavazzi, F., T. Jappelli and M. Pagano (2000), "Searching for Non-linear Effects of Fiscal Policy: Evidence from Industrial and Developing Countries", *European Economic Review*, Vol. 44, No. 7, pp. 1259-90.

IMF (2001), *Brazil: Report on Observance of Standards and Codes (ROSC), Fiscal Transparency Module*, Country Report No. 01/217, IMF, Washington, D.C.

IMF (2003), *World Economic Outlook*, IMF, September, IMF, Washington, D.C.

IMF (2005), *World Economic Outlook*, IMF, September, IMF, Washington, D.C.

Lane, P.R. (2003), "The Cyclical Behaviour of Fiscal Policy: Evidence from the OECD", *Journal of Public Economics*, Vol. 87, pp. 2661-75.

McDermott, J. and R.F. Wescott (1996), "An Empirical Analysis of Fiscal Adjustments", *IMF Staff Papers*, Vol. 43, No. 4, pp. 725–53.

Martner, R. and V. Tromben (2004a), "Tax Reforms and Fiscal Stabilisation in Latin American Countries", *Serie Gestión Pública*, No. 45, ILPES/ECLAC, Santiago.

Martner, R. and V. Tromben (2004b), "La Sostenibilidad de la Deuda Pública, el Efecto Bola de Nieve y el "Pecado Original"", *Serie Gestión Pública*, No. 46, ILPES/ECLAC, Santiago.

Mendoza, E.G. and P.M. Oviedo (2004), "Public Debt, Fiscal Solvency and Macroeconomic Uncertainty in Latin America: The Cases of Brazil, Colombia, Costa Rica, and Mexico", *NBER Working Papers*, No. 10637, NBER, Cambridge, MA.

Van Den Noord, P. (2000), "The Size and Role of Automatic Fiscal Stabilisers in the 1990s and Beyond", *OECD Economics Department Working Papers,* No. 230, OECD, Paris.

OECD (2003a), *Economic Outlook*, No. 74, OECD, Paris.

OECD (2003b), *OECD Economic Survey of Chile*, OECD, Paris.

OECD (2004), *OECD Economic Survey of Mexico*, OECD, Paris.

OECD (2005a), *OECD Economic Survey of Brazil*, OECD, Paris.

Perry, G. (2003), "Can Fiscal Rules Help Reduce Macroeconomic Volatility in the Latin America and Caribbean Region?", *Mimeo*, World Bank, Washington, D.C.

Reinhart, C., K. Rogoff and M. Savastano (2003), "Debt Intolerance," *Brookings Papers on Economic Activity*, Brookings Institution, pp. 1–62.

Rocha, F. and P. Picchetti (2003), "Fiscal adjustment in Brazil", *Revista Brasileira de Economia*, Vol. 57, No. 1, pp. 239-52.

Singh, A., A. Belaisch, C. Collyns, P. de Masi, R. Krieger, G. Meredith and R. Rennhack (2005), "Stabilization and Reform in Latin America: A Macroeconomic Perspective on the Experience Since the Early 1990s", *Occasional Paper*, No. 238, IMF, Washington, D.C.

Sorensen, B.E., L. Wu and O. Yosha (2001), "Output fluctuations and fiscal Policy: US State and local governments 1978-94", *European Economic Review*, Vol. 45.

Stein, E., E. Talvi and A. Grisanti (1999), "Institutional Arrangements and Fiscal Performance: The Latin American Experience", in James M. Poterba and Jurgen von Hagen (eds.), *Fiscal Institutions and Fiscal Performance*, University of Chicago Press, Chicago.

Talvi, E. and C.A. Vegh (2000), "Tax Base Variability and Procyclical Fiscal Policy", *NBER Working Paper*, No. 7499, NBER, Cambridge, MA.

Wodon, Q., N. Hicks, B. Ryan and G. Gonzalez (2000), "Are Governments Pro-Poor but Short-Sighted? Targeted and Social Spending for the Poor during Booms and Busts", mimeo, World Bank, Washington, D.C.

Chapter 2

Perspectives for fiscal adjustment in Latin America

Lisa M. Schineller,

Standard & Poor's

This chapter discusses the market's perception of fiscal adjustment in Latin America. It reviews the key methodological features used to determine a sovereign credit rating and assesses the fiscal performance of a number of Latin American credits. Several fiscal indicators are reported. A sovereign rating focuses only on a government's ability and willingness to repay debt on time and in full. Sovereign rating methodology is argued to be both quantitative and qualitative, incorporating an assessment of policy credibility, transparency and predictability. Fiscal policy plays a crucial role in credit rating analysis, including the fiscal authorities' ability and willingness to adjust policy to shocks or changing economic conditions.

Introduction

Standard & Poor's rates 16 sovereigns in Latin America, but only two countries, Chile and Mexico, have investment-grade ratings. Their stronger creditworthiness reflects their comparatively stronger fiscal positions in relation to the other Latin American countries, as well as other factors. The level of government debt does not *determine* a rating by itself. For example, Belgium has net general government debt of almost 90% of GDP and a "AA+" rating, while Ecuador's net debt of almost 40% of GDP is much lower, but so is its "CCC+" rating. These very different ratings reflect different political and institutional strengths, these countries' ability and willingness to adjust policy to shocks or changing economic conditions, and different policy track records, as well as fiscal flexibility, the structure of debt (the relative weight of domestic- as opposed to foreign currency-denominated securities, maturity structure, etc.), the depth of local capital markets, external vulnerabilities and the strength of the economy, among other determinants.

While sovereign analysis incorporates a variety of factors, a key focus is, obviously, on fiscal policy. Within the framework of Standard & Poor's sovereign fiscal criteria, this chapter will consider the various successes and challenges that remain in the fiscal area across Latin America. The chapter outlines aspects of Standard & Poor's methodology, compares various fiscal indicators and discusses strengths and weaknesses in fiscal institutions across the region. In comparing fiscal indicators, the chapter generally first considers Chile, Mexico, Brazil and Argentina (in order of descending rating level), and then other selected Latin American countries by rating category (Colombia, Costa Rica, Panama, Peru, Uruguay, Venezuela and Ecuador). The analysis spans the periods 1997-2000, 2001-04 and 2004 to compare recent and past trends.

Sovereign ratings and methodology

A sovereign rating is an opinion on a government's creditworthiness, not a recommendation to buy or sell a security or a prediction of the stability/volatility of a security price. As such, a sovereign rating reflects the ability and willingness of a government to repay debt on time and in full. It incorporates medium-term repayment prospects and aims to be robust through business, interest-rate, political and commodity-price cycles, as well as near-term market developments.

Standard & Poor's sovereign rating methodology is both quantitative and qualitative in nature. In addition to focusing on various data, it incorporates an assessment of political/institutional credibility, as well as the transparency and

CHALLENGES TO FISCAL ADJUSTMENT IN LATIN AMERICA – ISBN 9264022074 © OECD 2006

predictability of policy by current and future administrations. Vulnerability to internal/external shocks is affected by the country's economic structure, the consistency of the government's macroeconomic policy mix, the public/private sector external debt burdens and recent debt-servicing track records (Table 2.1).

Countries with investment-grade ratings have more resilient, predictable institutions, as well as stronger economic, fiscal and external positions. By definition, a speculative-grade credit is more vulnerable to internal and external shocks given a combination of its political and economic structures and institutions, as well as its fiscal, monetary and/or external vulnerabilities. By definition, Standard & Poor's is less confident about the ability and willingness of policymakers in a speculative-grade credit to effectively respond to shocks and to adjust policy in accordance with evolving economic conditions.

A sovereign rating reflects a confluence of factors with fiscal policy being a key component of credit quality. Standard & Poor's takes six main criteria into account when considering a sovereign rating: political risk, economic structure and growth prospects, fiscal policy/stability, monetary stability, external liquidity, and external public and private sector debt burdens. While a rating is forward-looking, the legacy of past policies does play a role, a key example being the nation's public debt burden.

Table 2.1. **Latin America: Foreign currency sovereign ratings**
As of November 2004

	S&P credit rating
Chile	A
Mexico	BBB-
El Salvador	BB+
Colombia	BB
Costa Rica	BB
Panama	BB
Peru	BB
Brazil	BB-
Guatemala	BB-
Uruguay	B
Venezuela	B
Bolivia	B-
Paraguay	B-
Ecuador	CCC+
Dominican Rep.	CC
Argentina	SD (Selected Default)

Source: Standard and Poor's.

The fiscal policy criteria

Standard & Poor's looks at the following fiscal indicators when analysing prospective fiscal policy: the current and projected path of budget balances (including expenditure and revenue flexibility), the current and projected level of government debt and interest burden, and off-budget and contingent liabilities. The analysis is based on fiscal indicators for the general government; namely, the central government (including the central bank), the middle-tier and local governments, the social security system and other government agencies. When such data are not readily available from official sources, estimates are compiled for comparative purposes. Non-financial and financial public enterprises are considered for potential contingent liabilities.

In assessing fiscal balances, Standard & Poor's employs stricter standards or benchmarks for countries that are officially dollarised or that have very limited monetary or exchange rate flexibility. In the region, this includes not only Panama, El Salvador and Ecuador, which are dollarised, but also Costa Rica and Uruguay. While implicit in the Standard & Poor's methodology before the Argentine default in 2001, the current criteria incorporate a more specific assessment of fiscal balances, should monetary/exchange rate policy autonomy be constrained. It is important to note that Standard & Poor's does not judge the merits of a fixed *versus* floating exchange-rate regime *per se*, but the rating aims to reflect the consistency, or lack thereof, of the country's macroeconomic policy mix. The combination of various moves towards floating exchange-rate regimes and the stabilisation of the real/nominal exchange rate, coupled with some improved fiscal effort in a number of Latin American countries, reflects a healthier, more consistent policy mix. For example, since the late 1990s, there have been moves towards more sustainable policy frameworks in Brazil, Colombia, Uruguay and post-crisis Argentina, with debt restructuring in the latter two countries.

Fiscal balances: Mixed record reflects rating divergences

In terms of fiscal balances, Chile clearly stands out demonstrating the strongest fiscal performance in the region (Figure 2.1), in line with its "A" rating. In Chile, the general government posted balanced budgets on average during 1997-2003, including a surplus of 2.2% of GDP in 2004. In Mexico, Brazil and Argentina, fiscal imbalances improved over the period 2001-04 compared to 1997-2000. However, fiscal positions in other "BB" and "B" Latin American credits remain fragile with some deterioration over the period 2001-04.

CHALLENGES TO FISCAL ADJUSTMENT IN LATIN AMERICA – ISBN 9264022074 © OECD 2006

Figure 2.1. **General government budget outcomes**
Headline budget balance in per cent of GDP

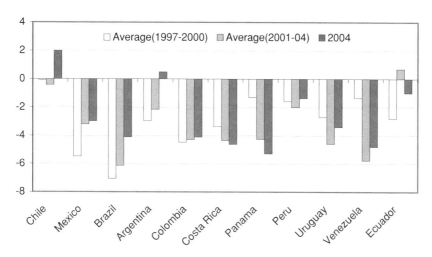

Source: Standard and Poor's.

Mexico had a legacy of relatively high deficits in the 1990s, averaging 5.5% of GDP during 1997-2000. Mexico's average deficit, however, declined to the neighbourhood of 3% of GDP during 2001-04, which contributed in part to its upgrade to "BBB-" in early 2002. For Mexico, Standard & Poor's uses the public sector balance as an approximation for the general government balance. Fiscal consolidation at the central government level has been important in bringing down the headline deficit, given the existence of off-budget expenditure commitments. Except for 2002, when the central government deficit reached 1.7% of GDP, the deficit averaged below 1% of GDP during the Fox administration. A progressive reduction in the costs associated with bank restructuring (from the 1994-95 Tequila crisis) has been offset by increases in off-budget infrastructure spending.

Until recently, Brazil's general government deficits have been high and volatile. Amid crises in 1999 and 2002, the headline budget deficit reached some 10% of GDP, given the depreciation of the *real*, the hike in interest rates needed to restore monetary and exchange rate stability, and the problematic structure of domestic debt. However, an improvement in public finances is expected in the near term owing to continued consolidation of the government's primary fiscal effort, coupled with a more stable exchange rate and the reduction in the share of US dollar-linked debt. This fiscal improvement was one of the factors that contributed to the upgrade of Brazil's ratings to "BB-" in late 2004.

In Argentina, fiscal performance worsened through 2001 when the headline budget deficit peaked at 6% of GDP in the midst of a severe economic crisis. The subsequent strengthening of public finances reflects an effort to control spending and the limited financing options available after the debt default. For 2004, the projected general government deficit of 0.7% of GDP incorporates some spending restraint and better-than-anticipated revenue performance, given the economic rebound, with windfall revenue being largely saved.

Other Latin American countries have a mixed fiscal track record, as reflected in their rating levels and outlooks. The fiscal positions of Colombia ("BB") and Peru ("BB") are improving. However, Panama's ("BB") and Costa Rica's ("BB") budget balances have deteriorated in recent years. Limited or no monetary flexibility has underpinned negative outlooks on these ratings, with policy effort to redress the fiscal imbalances being key to removing the negative outlooks. "B"-rated Uruguay had experienced significant fiscal deterioration until 2003-04 when the government accelerated fiscal adjustment amid crisis. The debt restructuring of 2003 altered expectations and permitted an economic recovery that strengthened fiscal performance in 2004, supported by some spending restraint. In Ecuador, the 1999 crisis, the debt restructuring of 2000 and dollarisation have been conducive to fiscal improvement. Nevertheless, the government has not used its oil revenue as effectively as it could. Similarly, Venezuela has not taken advantage of a favourable oil-price environment to reduce its fiscal imbalances.

Primary fiscal balances: Also a mixed performance

As part of its analysis of fiscal sustainability, Standard & Poor's assesses the primary fiscal effort undertaken by the government against that needed on the basis of the magnitude of the government's debt burden and prospects for economic growth and the level of real interest rates. In general, this is more important for lower-rated sovereigns, reflecting greater uncertainty about fiscal sustainability and their comparatively weak creditworthiness. In addition to having a bearing on the assessment of the prospective public debt trajectory, the primary surplus effort is an important determinant of access to capital market financing, which is another variable to monitor at the more precarious rating levels (and taken for granted for higher-rating credits). Likewise, the availability of financing from multilateral agencies often depends on compliance with primary and/or headline budget balance targets.

Given their investment-grade ratings, the discussion of a "minimum" or "needed" primary effort should not come into play when analysing Mexico or

CHALLENGES TO FISCAL ADJUSTMENT IN LATIN AMERICA – ISBN 9264022074 © OECD 2006

Figure 2.2. **General government primary budget balances**
In per cent of GDP

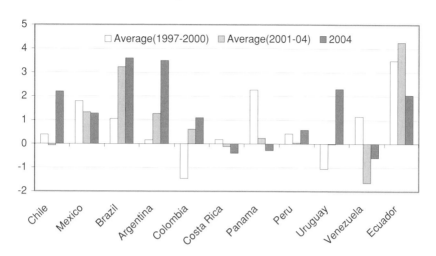

Source: Standard and Poor's.

Chile (Figure 2.2). However, the strengthening of Brazil's primary surplus effort has been a crucial component of the improved credibility of its fiscal policy. Brazil's general government primary surplus more than doubled from an average of 1.1% of GDP during 1997-2000 (beginning from a 1.1% of GDP deficit in 1997) to an average surplus of 3.2% of GDP during 2001-04, and 3.6% of GDP in 2004. Under considerable debate in the markets is the magnitude of the feasible and acceptable primary effort by the Argentine government to reduce its debt burden. Argentina's recent performance has been much stronger than initially expected: the general government budget surplus could be around 6% of GDP in 2004, higher than the government's stated commitment over the medium term. When debt restructuring is completed, and the magnitude of the debt burden is determined, the post-default rating Standard & Poor's assigns to Argentina will incorporate the actual expected primary fiscal effort in relation to what is "needed" given economic growth and real interest rate trends, among other parameters.

Just as the headline budget balances, primary efforts also vary across countries. Deteriorating primary budget balances against the magnitude of their debt burdens imply the need for the primary surplus effort to rise in Panama and Costa Rica. The primary budget balance has slowly risen in Colombia since the late 1990s, but additional effort is needed in response to rising spending on pensions. In Uruguay, the primary effort turnaround has been impressive over the past two years, but must rise even further. Given the country's high debt burden and limited growth prospects, favourable primary (and overall fiscal) performance, with some additional tightening of policy, is needed to ensure access to capital market and multilateral funding. Ecuador has run a primary effort higher than most other countries in the region in recent years, and its debt is also low compared with its peers. However, cash flow constraints and the policy of official dollarisation and limited access to capital markets and multilateral financing leave the government with no alternative policy option. Even with high oil prices, institutional weaknesses and a poor policy track record constrain the rating at a very low level.

Fiscal institutions and policy track record

Fiscal institutions and practices play an important role in analysing prospective fiscal performances, as does the government's policy track record. In general, investment-grade ratings reflect comparatively strong(er) institutions and greater predictability of policy, especially in the fiscal area. The recent trend in Latin America to legislate "fiscal responsibility" is laudable and a step towards fostering policy predictability. However, Standard & Poor's analyses potential improvements in fiscal policy and fiscal institutions not just by mere passage of a law, but also in terms of implementation and the establishment of a credible policy track record. Both Chile's and Mexico's investment-grade ratings reflect the comparatively strong predictability of fiscal policy and fiscal institutions, although neither country has a formal fiscal responsibility law. Brazil passed a fiscal responsibility law in 2000 that has contributed markedly to the development of a spirit, culture and general awareness of fiscal prudence across political parties and levels of government. While there remain some violations of the letter of the law, it has successfully contributed to improving fiscal performance at all levels of government, backed by market pressures as well.

Panama passed a fiscal responsibility law in 2002, which has not been respected in spirit or letter. The government that took office in September 2004 legislated a temporary suspension of the law, while aiming to bring balances back in line with the fiscal rule. Peru passed a fiscal responsibility law at the end of 1999, but one that has not been systematically complied with, leading to its revision. The government also missed the fiscal targets established with the International Monetary Fund (IMF) during a number of years. However, Peru's fiscal track record has strengthened and its goal of attaining a deficit of 1% of GDP for the non-financial public sector in 2005 is within reach. Colombia's track record of revising its fiscal targets with the IMF weakens credibility in its budgetary planning process. However, the government passed a fiscal responsibility law in 2003 and is moving towards strengthening the budget planning process.

CHALLENGES TO FISCAL ADJUSTMENT IN LATIN AMERICA – ISBN 9264022074 © OECD 2006

Chile stands out in the region as having a prudent fiscal policy framework and established a strong track record, as evidenced by its highest rating in Latin America. Chile is the only Latin American country with a low enough debt burden to effectively pursue counter-cyclical fiscal policy, as discussed by Luiz de Mello and Nanno Mulder in Chapter 1. In 1987, Chile created a copper stabilisation fund to save copper revenue windfalls and moderate fiscal contractions during economic slowdowns. Such funds are an appropriate policy buffer in nations dependent on commodity revenue. Chile's policy track record strengthened further with the adoption of a fiscal rule, beginning in 2001, with the aim of achieving a structural budget surplus of 1% of GDP. This degree of fiscal policy maturity is not found elsewhere in Latin America. The separation of political interests from the budget process includes an independent commission to estimate potential GDP growth and medium-term copper prices that are used to calibrate revenue projections. Last year provided a good test as to how the policy performs under higher-than-expected growth and copper prices, which led to increased fiscal savings. The government posted a budget surplus of over 2% of GDP in 2004 consistent with abidance by the structural surplus rule.

Mexico's fiscal track record and policy framework suggest that commitment to prudent policy has become mainstream, as in Chile, and across political party lines. This enhanced policy credibility was a key component of the upgrade to "BBB-", or investment grade, by Standard & Poor's in February 2002. While not having a formal fiscal responsibility law, Mexico's track record of prudent policy adjustment has been tested under political transition. Successive governments have followed a policy of reducing central government spending in line with revenue shortfalls; the budget incorporates automatic spending cuts in line with fluctuations in revenue.

In general, a comparatively centralised fiscal framework has been more closely associated with fiscal prudence, at least in Latin America. Unlike other countries in the region, Mexico's intergovernmental fiscal relations have not compromised fiscal prudence. Fiscal adjustment has been shared across the different levels of government, because local governments raise little of their own revenue and rely on transfers from the central government. These transfers are rules-based and depend on revenue performance at the central government level. As Mexican local governments have become more interested in policy autonomy and in raising their own budget financing, the government established credit controls for bank lending to local governments (loans now require ratings by two independent agencies), although implementation is yet to be fully tested.

Despite its investment-grade rating, Mexico does not yet have a sufficient degree of flexibility to pursue counter-cyclical fiscal policy. Off-budget spending, most notably for failed banks and infrastructure projects (PIDIREGAS), and reliance on revenue from the state-owned oil company (PEMEX), which could be compromised by the need to increase investment, imply that additional fiscal improvement is required at the general government level over the medium-term before counter-cyclical fiscal policy can be considered an effective policy option. In addition, the practice of effectively saving higher-than-expected revenue, specifically oil receipts, has yet to be secured.

Brazil's fiscal institutions are at least as strong as those of its peer credits, having strengthened significantly since the late 1990s, culminating with the passage of a fiscal responsibility law in 2000. Fiscal performance has also been bolstered by Brazil's consistent meeting, or surpassing, the primary budget targets established with the IMF since 1998. Note that Brazil does not have headline budget balance targets, which it would likely not have met in crisis years. In addition, Brazil's three-year budget guidelines law indicates the likely fiscal stance over a three-year time horizon. Owing to growing awareness of the need for fiscal responsibility, it includes an analysis of essentially downside risks to the macroeconomic and budgetary projections. Each level of government also presents a four-year public spending/investment plan. In combination, these policies have led to a perception of more credible and responsible fiscal policymaking.

Not unlike other countries in Latin America, many provisions in Brazil's 1988 Constitution had significant negative fiscal implications, including the mandated transfer of revenue to the states and municipalities without commensurate expenditure responsibilities. However, Brazil's fiscal federalism arrangements have become sound(er) since the late 1990s. A significant deterioration of state finances prompted various bailouts by the federal government in the early 1990s. The federal rescheduling of sub-national government debts during 1997-2000, the passage of the fiscal responsibility law and the closure of the states' financial institutions have been effective to date in generating an important contribution by the sub-national governments to fiscal adjustment. These agreements allow for only limited borrowing and, on balance, have been respected, despite intermittent pressure by the states to loosen some of the constraints.

Argentina's fiscal institutions are weak in relation to most rated sovereigns. The protracted nature of Argentina's debt rescheduling with private-sector creditors and tensions with the IMF over policy commitments have eroded the institutional improvement that occurred during the early 1990s. A much stronger-than-anticipated fiscal performance in 2003-04 reflects the economic rebound that has buoyed tax revenue, as well as expenditure restraint.

CHALLENGES TO FISCAL ADJUSTMENT IN LATIN AMERICA – ISBN 9264022074 © OECD 2006

However, the increase in the revenue-to-GDP ratio is unlikely to be permanent, hence the need for reform to bolster medium-term fiscal performance. Progress on longer-term fiscal reform has been limited, with no real advance on pursuing a solid fiscal responsibility law, putting in place budgetary mechanisms to ensure fiscal discipline at the provincial level, or reforming the tax-sharing agreements (*coparticipaciones*) between the central and provincial governments, as discussed by Oscar Centrangolo in his comments on Pablo Guidotti's chapter. In addition, uncertainty remains about effective policy implementation. Establishing a track record will be the key to restoring credibility.

Revenue flexibility

In assessing prospective fiscal performance, Standard & Poor's considers revenue flexibility and the ability to adjust (namely, increase) collections to changing economic conditions and fiscal needs, as well as the adequacy and efficiency of the tax system. Latin America suffers from comparatively narrower revenue bases in relation to higher-rated and/or industrialised countries (Figure 2.3).

The exception, however, is Brazil, with a general government revenue base of 38% of GDP, and tax revenue accounting for about 35% of GDP in 2004. Brazil's tax burden rose from 29% of GDP in the mid-1990s, as the government increased taxes to support the generation of primary budget surpluses. Brazil's tax regime, while comparatively effective in collecting taxes, is very complicated and poses a large burden on the formal economy. In the near term, it would be important to reform the tax system so as to reduce distortions. Once the debt-to-GDP ratio has declined, lowering the tax burden in line with a reduction in expenditure commitments would prove more supportive of investment and conducive to sustainable, long-term growth.

Chile's general government revenue has remained relatively stable at about 23% of GDP, with taxes accounting for around 18% of GDP. While these revenue bases are lower than similarly-rated credits, whose revenue accounts for an average 42% of GDP, they are adequate for Chile's fiscal burden. In addition, Chile's tax collection is the most effective among Latin American credits. By contrast, Mexico's revenue base is very small and narrow, and tax administration is comparatively inefficient. Central government revenue is around 18% of GDP, much lower than peer credits whose revenue averages 32% of GDP. Mexico's tax take is close to 10% of GDP, excluding oil-related revenue. Mexico has struggled to increase and broaden its tax base, facing strong political resistance. An important policy goal would be to broaden the value-added tax base since one-half of the potential tax base is zero-rated or exempt, as discussed by Rogelio Arellano and Fausto Hernández in Chapter 6. Other things equal, improved creditworthiness and a stronger fiscal framework could depend on the ability to increase/broaden the tax base to satisfy pressing social and infrastructure needs over the medium term.

Figure 2.3. **General government revenue and tax productivity**

A. Revenue, in per cent of GDP

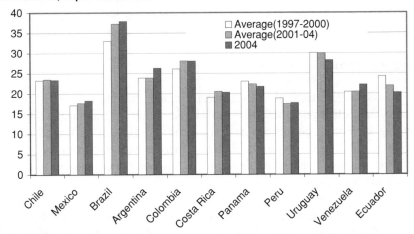

B. Revenue productivity, 2001[1]

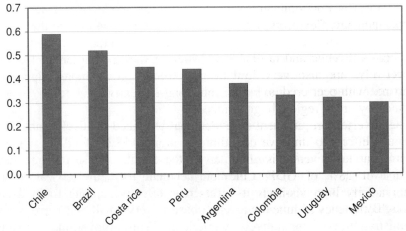

1.   VAT revenue in per cent of consumption divided by the standard VAT rate, 2001.
Source: Standard and Poor's.and IMF.

CHALLENGES TO FISCAL ADJUSTMENT IN LATIN AMERICA – ISBN 9264022074 © OECD 2006

Problems of weak tax administration and enforcement have constrained Argentina's fiscal performance since the 1990s, when the government granted tax amnesties periodically. Argentina's general government revenue base averaged 24% of GDP during the late 1990s. Tax revenue, however, averaged a much lower 15-17% of GDP, suggesting that there is room for improvement in collection, although not as much as in Mexico. In 2004, tax revenue was buoyant, reflecting some improvement in tax administration and collection effort, and mainly strong economic recovery and the introduction of distortionary taxes on exports (including oil) and financial transactions. Dependency on an increasingly narrow tax base and on inefficient instruments, along with increased informal economic activity since the crisis, tends to undermine the sustainability of Argentina's tax base over the medium term.

Elsewhere in the region, the governments of Costa Rica and Panama are pursuing tax reform to broaden the tax base against a background of numerous loopholes and/or the absence of taxation in many sectors of the economy. While overall general government revenue in these countries is between 20-22% of GDP, the ratio of tax revenue to GDP is much lower, around 12% in Costa Rica and a mere 9% for the central government in Panama. Reform to increase the tax base by 2.5% of GDP has proven politically difficult in Costa Rica, being under discussion in Congress for several years. In Panama, the new government aims to bring some of the more buoyant sectors of the economy, currently exempt from taxation, into the tax base. In both countries, prospects for reform are likely to have credit implications. Passage and effective implementation of solid reform is important given a recent deterioration in public finances and limited monetary flexibility.

Peru's revenue and tax bases of almost 18% of GDP and 13% of GDP, respectively, are also very low in view of its social spending needs and compared with peer credits. Future reform includes reducing the tax incentives granted by the regional governments. However, Peru's tax regime is comparatively more efficient than those of other countries in the region. In Uruguay, efforts to improve tax administration advanced in late 2003; central government tax revenue is about 15% of GDP, against central government revenue of 28% of GDP. Colombia's revenue base of 28% of GDP is comparatively high vis-à-vis its peers. Its tax base is about 20% of GDP, although efficiency is quite low.

Financial transactions taxes

A recent trend in the region has been to use distortionary financial transactions taxes (Argentina, Brazil, Colombia, Peru and Venezuela) since they are easy to collect and capture activity in the informal economy. The benefit of these taxes is that they can – and are being used by the authorities – to combat tax evasion through the cross-checking of tax declarations. In fact, some nations, such as Peru, plan to reduce the rate over time or permit payments to be deducted against other tax liabilities. All things equal, the use of less distortionary taxes would be preferable, given their detrimental impact on economic competitiveness and growth prospects. However, at lower rates, where revenue generation is often crucial to underpin stronger fiscal performance, the quality of taxation becomes of second-order importance.

Dependency on volatile commodity revenues

For countries that are dependent on commodity-related revenue, the creation of stabilisation funds enhances revenue flexibility over the business cycle, in addition to generating savings for future generations, as in many countries in the Middle East. In Latin America, only Chile has a stabilisation fund that operates effectively and smoothes copper revenue over business/commodity cycles. While Mexico has a fund that contains monies from oil revenue that exceeds the budget's reference price, most of these funds are actually spent each year according to a formula, thus rendering fiscal policy pro-cyclical, as discussed by Rogelio Arellano and Fausto Hernández in Chapter 6, as well as Bénédicte Larre in her comments. While the fiscal responsibility law of 2002 created an oil fund in Ecuador, such that 70% of the monies be used for debt buybacks/reduction, the funds have been used to date essentially to finance the deficit. In Venezuela, where 50% of government revenue stems from oil, there is no effective oil stabilisation fund.

Expenditure flexibility

Expenditure flexibility is particularly crucial when assessing a government's ability to adjust its finances in the face of challenging economic conditions. Countries at lower rating levels, which includes most Latin American credits, have limited expenditure flexibility, with payroll, pensions, interest payments and other "earmarked" items accounting for a large share of spending. Unfortunately, in combination with tight fiscal positions at the lower-rating level, this implies limited opportunity for increasing economically important social, human capital and physical capital expenditures that would tend to raise productivity and enhance growth prospects over the longer term.

Chile and Mexico have comparatively more expenditure flexibility than other Latin American credits, which is not surprising given their stronger creditworthiness. Non-discretionary spending accounts for 50-55% and 60% of central government revenue in Chile and Mexico, respectively. On the other hand, around 80% of Brazil's central government revenue goes towards payroll, pensions, interest payments and other mandated spending. Before its default and the cessation of interest payments, 60-65% of Argentine central government revenue went to cover payroll, pensions and interest payments. Inflexibility was even higher, at around 95% of revenue, if transfers to the provinces were included. In Colombia, around two-thirds of central government revenue goes towards wages, pensions and interest payments, but non-discretionary spending also includes mandated transfers to local governments. In Costa Rica and Ecuador, non-discretionary spending captures 75% of central government revenue, while in Panama and Uruguay the figure is close to 90%.

For most of Latin America, improving expenditure flexibility requires a concerted political effort. It entails overcoming cumbersome constitutions that legislate aspects of fiscal policy, implementing administrative reform that includes payroll restraint, working towards a sustainable reduction in indebtedness, and, in many instances, implementing pension reform.

Pension reform

Pension reform has yielded mixed results across Latin America. While the privatisation of pension regimes and a shift away from pay-as-you-go, government-sponsored systems has been successful to date in Chile and Mexico, it failed to stem fiscal imbalances elsewhere in the region. Many governments underestimated the transition costs involved in reform, as discussed by Pablo Guidotti in Chapter 3, and/or have inadequately adjusted spending to accommodate these transition costs, which proved to be a destabilising fiscal burden in Argentina, Uruguay and Bolivia. Large pay-as-you-go fiscal imbalances still weigh on expenditure flexibility in Brazil, Panama and Colombia, where further pension reform could improve creditworthiness. Pension reform is clearly needed in these systems to better align entitlements with contributions, but whether a complete shift to a privatised individual account scheme is appropriate is unclear.

Debt burden

Although not the sole determinant of a sovereign rating, as noted previously, the size of government debt (net of liquid assets available for debt repayment) as a share of GDP does play an important role in assessing fiscal sustainability and creditworthiness. Investment-grade Chile and Mexico have among the lowest debt ratios in Latin America, at around 20 and 40% of GDP, respectively (Figure 2.4) Brazil's net general government debt-to-GDP ratio is higher at almost 52% of GDP in 2004, and Argentina's pre-debt restructuring was around 140% of GDP.

Figure 2.4. **General government debt and interest burden**

☐ Average(1997-2000) ▦ Average(2001-04) ■ 2004

A. General government debt, in per cent of GDP

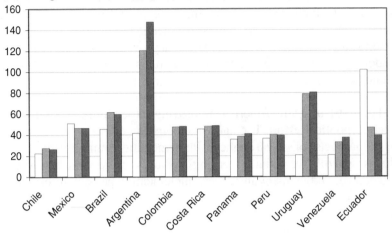

B. Interest burden, in per cent of general government revenue

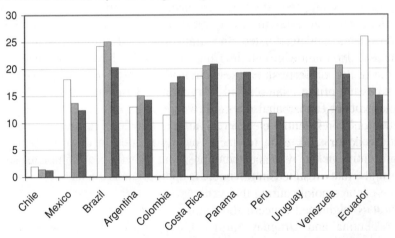

Source: Standard and Poor's.

For "BB"-rated Colombia, Costa Rica, Panama and Peru, net debt stands at between 40-50% of GDP. Much lower-rated Ecuador and Venezuela also have net debt ratios at around 40% of GDP, with their ratings reflecting other weaknesses, particularly political and institutional, as well as the questionable sustainability of their macroeconomic policy mixes. Ecuador restructured its debt in 2000 with a 40% reduction in face value. In contrast, Uruguay has a

CHALLENGES TO FISCAL ADJUSTMENT IN LATIN AMERICA – ISBN 9264022074 © OECD 2006

significant debt ratio, at around 80% of GDP, and the 2003 debt restructuring did not include a reduction in principal. Expectations of Uruguay's commitment to keeping fiscal policy on a prudent track would permit a gradual reduction in debt over time; comparatively stronger institutions and policy predictability support its debt at the "B" rating level.

With regard to the magnitude of a government's debt burden, credit rating analysis considers not only the debt-to-GDP ratio, but also the general government interest burden and the composition of public debt. In general, Latin American sovereigns have high interest burdens compared with other similarly-rated credits, the marked exception being Chile, whose general government interest burden is lower than that of its peer credits. Even Mexico's 12% interest-revenue ratio is almost double that of other credits in the "BBB" category. Brazil's interest burden has settled at around 20% of revenue, but has spiked much higher during periods of financial stress. Argentina's interest burden reached 15% of revenue in 2004, although it was not servicing 60% of its debt. In recent years, the interest burden in Colombia, Costa Rica, Panama, Uruguay and Venezuela rose to around 20% of revenue, a comparatively high ratio. Ecuador's interest-revenue ratio declined toward 15%, a drop that in part reflects debt relief.

The composition and maturity structure of government debt also contributes to Standard & Poor's fiscal analysis. The composition of debt itself can have important effects on the level of indebtedness relative to GDP and on the volatility of interest payments relative to revenue, and hence on fiscal balances. A prime example is how the problematic composition of Brazil's domestic debt exacerbated the debt dynamics during the 2002 crisis, ahead of the nation's presidential election. Given the then high share of debt indexed to the US dollar and also to local overnight interest rates, the significant depreciation of the *real* and the subsequent monetary policy response to hike overnight rates resulted in an increase in Brazil's debt-to-GDP ratio of about 13 percentage points during that year. The very short tenor of Brazil's domestic debt also heightened concern about rollover risk in 2002. The recent debt crises in Argentina and Uruguay further highlight the vulnerabilities created by issuing debt in foreign currency in countries with semi or fixed exchange-rate regimes undermined by an inconsistent policy mix. Debt-to-GDP ratios more than doubled in these crisis situations as a result of currency depreciation.

A sovereign should ideally issue debt at long tenors, at fixed interest rates and in its own currency. Latin American nations do not enjoy this luxury. Even "A"-rated Chile has 85% of its debt denominated in US dollars, as noted by Luiz de Mello and Nanno Mulder in Chapter 1. In recent years, Mexico's prudent liability management, aided by pension reform that supports demand for long-term debt placements in local currency, has served to reduce fiscal vulnerability. The government has lengthened the domestic yield curve with placements of 20 years' maturity. While still comparatively short, the average domestic tenor of 2½ years has doubled since 2001, and 40% of domestically issued/locally held central government debt is at fixed rates.

Brazil has made significant progress in reducing the share of US dollar-indexed debt from a peak of just over 40% of domestic debt in 2002 to under 10% at the end of 2004. However, with about 40% of domestic debt maturing within a 12-month period and over 50% of securities indexed to the overnight interest rate, much room remains for improvement in Brazil's debt structure. Such weaknesses in debt composition span the region.

Contingent and other potential liabilities

In addition to assessing fiscal balances, fiscal flexibility and a sovereign's debt burden, the analysis of the fiscal underpinnings of credit rating incorporates estimates of potential contingent liabilities to the government. In Latin America, debt burdens have systematically been compromised by off-budget, debt-creating operations. Chile is estimated to have lower contingent liabilities than the rest of sovereigns rated in Latin America.

In general, off-budget quasi-fiscal activities, as well as explicit or implicit guarantees by the government, are considered when estimating contingent liabilities. Recognition of debt arising from judicial rulings and other off-budget spending in various countries, such as Brazil and Argentina, contributed to important increases in their respective debt burdens. Recognition of debt in Argentina during 1993-2001 amounted to some 13% of GDP. In Brazil, the recognition of fiscal "skeletons" added about 10% of GDP to the debt burden during 1996-2003.

Standard & Poor's takes a cautious view of excluding public-sector investment from the fiscal targets. Such behaviour presents the risk that off-budget and/or unsupervised spending of a potentially more questionable nature may not be unaccounted for. The same reasoning could hold for guarantees and spending commitments associated with public-private partnerships (PPPs), should they be established without sufficient fiscal safeguards. Since the budget balance and the debt data are for the general government, an assessment of the potential drain on public finances posed by poorly-managed state-owned enterprises is also considered in credit-rating analysis. Pension liabilities are included in the assessment of fiscal balances. The financial sector may present another important contingent liability

CHALLENGES TO FISCAL ADJUSTMENT IN LATIN AMERICA – ISBN 9264022074 © OECD 2006

Table 2.2. **Potential contingent liabilities**

	Estimated NPL peaks (in %)	Credit to the private sector and non-financial public enterprises (in % of GDP, 2004)	Cost (in % of GDP)
Chile	10-20	64	7-14
Colombia	15-30	25	4-8
Panama	15-30	86	13-26
Brazil	25-40	33	8-13
Costa Rica	25-40	32	8-13
Mexico	25-40	16	4-6
Peru	25-40	21	5-8
Uruguay	25-40	42	10-17
Venezuela	35-50	9	3-5
Argentina	50-75	26	13-20
Ecuador	50-75	22	11-17

Source: Standard & Poor's and IMF.

for the government. As seen in numerous countries within and beyond Latin America, governments have been called upon to bail out large banks and/or the banking system as a whole. To estimate this risk, Standard & Poor's projects a scenario of peak non-performing loans (NPL) that could result from a "deep-recession" environment, given its assessment of the strengths and weaknesses of the nation's financial system (Table 2.2). Coupled with the extent of financial intermediation, the potential cost to the sovereign is calculated.

Future challenges and policies to improve creditworthiness

With the vast majority of Latin American sovereigns rated by Standard & Poor's in the speculative-grade category, there is ample opportunity for significant improvement in fiscal policy and fiscal institutions in the region. In addition to running tighter budget balances and reducing debt levels, improved fiscal flexibility is important. Most nations could benefit from broader revenue bases to support widespread pressure for increasing efficient, well-targeted and productive government spending, such as on physical, social and human capital accumulation. In addition, less distorting tax regimes would contribute to making these economies more efficient. Reduced expenditure rigidities via politically difficult pension reform, payroll restraint and the elimination of widespread earmarking in many countries could support increased ability to adjust spending as needed under unforeseen stress scenarios.

The establishment of prudent fiscal rules and norms, as well as transparent decision-making processes through the enactment of well-designed fiscal responsibility legislation, should increase policy predictability, as could the creation of stabilisation funds for commodity-dependent sovereigns. However, the development of a strong policy track record is crucial to gaining confidence. Entrenching prudent fiscal behaviour and norms is key not only at the central government level, but also throughout the public sector, given current patterns of devolution of fiscal responsibilities to local governments. Finally, debt management practices aimed at lengthening tenor, issuing securities denominated in local currency and at fixed interest rates, while taking time and part of overall capital market deepening, are important to reduce the vulnerability of debt stocks and interest burdens.

CHALLENGES TO FISCAL ADJUSTMENT IN LATIN AMERICA – ISBN 9264022074 © OECD 2006

Comments

Patrick Lenain,

OECD Economics Department

Credit rating agencies and information asymmetry

The fact that emerging markets are subject to information asymmetry is well established in the empirical literature. Issuers of emerging market debt are not required by market overseers to provide detailed economic and financial reports. Faced with high costs for acquiring information, most market participants prefer to follow supposedly better-informed investors, such as large institutional investors. This has been associated with the occurrence of "herd behaviour", contagion across countries and sudden capital flow reversals (Kräussl, 2003).

Thus, improving the transparency and quality of information is an important step towards strengthening international finance. Together with data dissemination standards, credit rating agencies can play a critical role in this respect. By assessing the creditworthiness of sovereign borrowers, rating agencies provide investors with the tools needed to make well-informed decisions. Thus, in principle, they can help to reduce adverse selection, steering investors towards creditworthy governments and away from fragile borrowers. Ratings can also lead market participants in the right direction, helping to cool off euphoria during periods of boom and to attenuate pessimism during periods of bust – if so warranted.

Several authors, however, doubt that rating agencies play this role effectively. They argue that these agencies tend to follow, rather than lead, market trends. Reisen (2003), for instance, finds that ratings fail to predict currency crisis and criticise rating agencies for having downgraded sovereign borrowers after the occurrence of crises, rather than before. This claim is based on a wide definition of the rating agencies' mandate, which typically includes the prediction of currency crises. If a narrower (and more accurate) definition of sovereign ratings is used – the probability of sovereign bond defaults – rating agencies appear apt to perform their task. Reinhart (2002) correctly tests whether credit ratings are good predictors of debt defaults, but she uses a data sample that includes defaults on the reimbursement of commercial bank credits, rather than defaults on sovereign bonds.

My comments adopt a different angle. Rather than discussing the predictive value of credit ratings, they examine qualitatively whether ratings contribute to reducing information asymmetry in the case of the Latin American borrowers examined by Lisa Schineller. For this purpose, two questions are asked: do rating agencies lead or follow market trends? And do ratings bring valuable information to the market?

Do credit ratings lead or follow market trends?

The intuition that rating agencies follow market trends is not implausible. Rating agencies could decide to upgrade borrowers when they benefit from large capital inflows and downgrade those suffering from large capital outflows. In this regard, it is worrying that rating agencies made a record number of upgrades shortly after a wave of optimism regarding emerging market prospects. Standard & Poor's raised 27% of its ratings in 2004, an unprecedented amount since it resumed assigning sovereign ratings in 1975 (Standard & Poor, 2005). In Latin America, the agency upgraded the sovereign debts of Brazil, Chile, Paraguay, Peru, Uruguay and Venezuela by one notch. It did not downgrade any major sovereign borrower in the region. The troubling fact is that this series of upgrades followed a period of market optimism, as illustrated by the fall of interest rate spreads on Latin American sovereign debt (Figure 2.5).[1] The sequencing of these two movements is worrying: at first glance, it could suggest that rating agencies just followed the optimism of market participants.

Rating agencies, however, remain cautious about the quality of Latin American sovereign debts. As Lisa Schineller's chapter reminds us, Latin American sovereign borrowers have a "mixed track record". The region includes a wide variety of credit ratings, ranging from the strong performance of Chile (rated "A") to the selective default of Argentina on certain classes of its obligations (rated "SD"). Despite recent upgrades, many countries in the region continue to have fragile debt servicing capacity: only two sovereign borrowers are regarded as "investment grade" (Chile and Mexico), while all the other rated sovereign borrowers are seen as having "significant speculative characteristics" due to inherent uncertainties (including Brazil and Peru).

CHALLENGES TO FISCAL ADJUSTMENT IN LATIN AMERICA – ISBN 9264022074 © OECD 2006

Figure 2.5. Interest spreads on Latin American sovereign debt, 2002-05

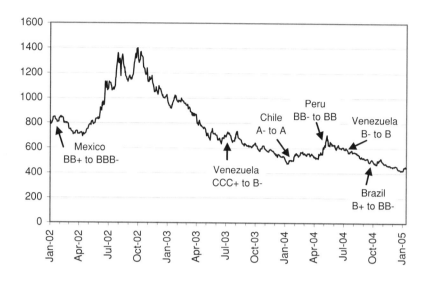

Source: JP Morgan EMBI+ for Latin America, and Standard and Poor's.

Lisa Schineller rightly stresses that several countries are still suffering from weak fiscal and debt management frameworks. Despite recent improvements, many of the countries have large and volatile budget deficits. They have narrow tax bases, which tend to fluctuate following commodity price cycles, and face large demands for public expenditure. Outstanding government debt stocks vary across countries, but are substantial and perhaps above prudent levels in some cases. This cautious assessment seems to have been overlooked by market participants in their search for yields in an environment of ample global liquidity. Thus, vigilance is called for.

Do credit ratings bring new information to the market?

In order to reduce information asymmetry, credit ratings need to provide new valuable information. If they merely reflect publicly-available information already incorporated in current market conditions, ratings will be ignored by investors or worse, they will exacerbate market trends. To be valuable, credit ratings need to reflect information unavailable to market participants and react rapidly to new developments. In this regard, the importance of providing an overall assessment of fiscal trends, rather than a narrow evaluation of the central government budget, cannot be stressed enough. Indeed, past emerging market crisis occurred unexpectedly in part because critical information on underlying fiscal developments was overlooked.

A typical example in this respect is the large exchange-rate exposure builtup by the Thai banking sector before the Asian crisis. Banks were borrowing in foreign currency and lending in domestic currency in large magnitudes, leading to a potentially damaging currency mismatch (Williamson, 2004). Although the banking sector is not part of the general government, most countries come to the rescue of banks that are too-large-to-fail and such financial risks should therefore be considered as a potential contingent government liability. This has prompted the IMF to integrate a Financial Sector Assessment Programme in its surveillance activity.

A second example is the accumulation of payment arrears by governments in transition economies, particularly Russia and Ukraine, as a way to ease budget deficits on a cash basis. In 1996-97, governments allowed wage and pension arrears to build up so as to avoid higher borrowing, which would have signalled a deterioration in the public finances. Although the accumulation of payment arrears was unsustainable, it masked the deterioration of the fiscal situation. A third example relates to the operation of fiscal federalism frameworks, with public expenditure obligations being transferred to lower levels of governments without the resources required, as occurred in Argentina before the 2001 financial crisis.

Getting the full picture in an environment of asymmetric information can be difficult and costly. In a comparative study of the resources spent by rating agencies in developed and developing countries, Ferri (2004) concludes that they allocate fewer resources to emerging market issuers than to OECD issuers. Lisa Schineller, by contrast, appears to go after the full picture, taking off-budget liabilities seriously, including explicit and implicit government guarantees, liabilities of state-owned companies, future pension burdens and potential non-performing loans accumulated by the financial sector. Let us hope that this effort indeed succeeds in providing a broad assessment of possible sources of fiscal stress.

Note

1. According to the EMBI+ spread index for Latin America.

CHALLENGES TO FISCAL ADJUSTMENT IN LATIN AMERICA – ISBN 9264022074 © OECD 2006

Bibliography

Ferri, G. (2004), "More Analysts, Better Ratings: Do Rating Agencies Invest Enough in Less Developed Countries?", *Journal of Applied Economics*, Vol. 7, No. 1, pp. 77-98.

Kräussl, R. (2003), "Do Credit Rating Agencies Add to the Dynamics of Emerging Market Crises?", *Working Paper*, No. 2003/18, Center for Financial Studies, Frankfurt.

Reinhart, C.H. (2002), "Default, Currency Crises and Sovereign Credit Ratings", *NBER Working Paper*, No. 8738, NBER, Cambridge, MA.

Reisen, H. (2003), "Ratings since the Asian Crisis", *Working Paper*, No. 214, OECD Development Centre, Paris.

Standard & Poor's (2005), "Sovereign Upgrades Set Record in 2004", Ratings Direct, New York.

Williamson, J. (2004), "The Years of Emerging Market Crises: A Review of Feldstein", *Journal of Economic Literature*, Vol. 42, No. 3, pp. 822-37.

Chapter 3

Argentina's fiscal policy in the 1990s: A tale of skeletons and sudden stops

Pablo E. Guidotti,

Universidad Torcuato di Tella

This chapter discusses fiscal adjustment in Argentina. It argues that the deterioration of the public debt dynamics prior to the 2001 crisis was due predominantly to the costs borne by the budget associated with the pension reform implemented in the early 1990s, the refinancing at market rates of the debt that had been restructured at concessionary rates under the Brady deal in 1992, and the recognition of previously unrecorded liabilities (fiscal "skeletons"). Instead of being perceived by the markets as instrumental in improving Argentina's fiscal accounts over the long term, despite its associated short-term costs, pension reform is argued to have contributed to the deterioration of investors' perception of debt sustainability in an environment of macroeconomic volatility and financial crises in other emerging market economies.

Introduction

Argentina's saga of success and trauma under Convertibility remains one of the most heatedly debated events in the country's recent economic history. On the one hand, by adopting in the early 1990s a quasi currency-board arrangement – called Convertibility – Argentina was able to sustain a period of rapid economic expansion, grounded on both the return of macroeconomic stability and the implementation of an ambitious agenda of structural reform and deregulation. On the other hand, despite its initial success, economic growth stalled after the Russian default in mid-1998. After a protracted recession, the Convertibility regime ended in 2001 in a crisis of unprecedented depth, characterised by devaluation, widespread default on public and private debts, financial turmoil and a cumulative drop in output of almost 15% in 2001 and 2002.

The origin and causes of the 2001 debacle are at the core of the current policy debate. For some analysts, the fixed exchange-rate regime that underpinned Convertibility contained in its rigidity the seeds of its own destruction, despite having allowed the Argentine economy to recover from hyperinflation and grow at unprecedented rates for a good number of years before its collapse. For others, still convalescent from several decades of macroeconomic mismanagement, Argentina fell victim of an unusual sequence of external shocks plaguing emerging market economies in the second half of the 1990s, in particular the capital market crises in Asia and Russia, the sharp decline in commodity prices, the strong appreciation of the US dollar and the successive devaluations in Mexico and Brazil. Finally, for many observers it was not the exchange-rate regime *per se* the centre of Argentina's problems but its lax fiscal policy that, the argument goes, allowed the public debt to balloon to unsustainable levels. Furthermore, as dollarisation was widespread, devaluation and default became intertwined from the point of view of investors.

In this chapter, I will not attempt to develop a comprehensive analysis of the causes of the collapse of the Convertibility regime in 2001, an issue that already attracted the attention of several analysts, notably Mussa (2002), Perry and Servén (2003) and Calvo, Izquierdo and Talvi (2002).[1] Rather, my narrower objective is to re-examine the role of fiscal policy in the 1990s in light of three crucial policy decisions taken at the beginning of the decade; namely, the conclusion of the Brady debt restructuring, the recognition of pre-existing arrears with pensioners and suppliers, and the privatisation of the pension system, while considering the restrictions imposed on debt sustainability by the capital market volatility experienced by emerging markets in the second half of the decade. In this sense, the analysis undertaken here can be viewed as

CHALLENGES TO FISCAL ADJUSTMENT IN LATIN AMERICA – ISBN 9264022074 © OECD 2006

complementary to the literature cited above and as a step towards fulfilling the more ambitious task of elucidating the full extent of the 2001 debacle.

The conclusion of the analysis is that these three policy decisions taken together amounted to a large fiscal bet, encouraged by the optimism that prevailed in capital markets at the beginning of the decade. Given the dominant role that liquidity considerations would have played after the crises in Asia and Russia, the kind of fiscal dynamics that emerged in the remainder of the decade left fiscal policy effectively with little room for manoeuvre, despite the government's efforts to contain expenditure. In this sense, the analysis presented in this chapter contrasts sharply with the conventional view that fiscal management was irresponsible at the time. Moreover, the extent to which liquidity considerations affected debt sustainability was not fully understood neither by the authorities nor the International Monetary Fund.[2]

Fiscal policy in Latin America in the 1990s: General considerations[3]

The 1990s was a remarkable decade, when emerging market economies experienced the initial euphoria of globalisation as well as the uncertainties and anxieties brought about by the contagion associated with the financial crises in Mexico and, later, in Asia, Russia and Brazil. The intensity of these experiences – with Latin America being no exception – motivated important policy discussions. In particular, while policies focused initially on taming inflation, the capital market crises of the mid-to-late 1990s turned the focus of analysis to debt sustainability and the development of instruments to deal with financial volatility.

For most countries in Latin America the advent of globalisation coincided with the end of a decade-long struggle with macroeconomic turmoil and debt default. The signing of the Brady deal allowed credit-constrained economies to start afresh a new relationship with international capital markets at a time when the supply of foreign capital to emerging markets in general was about to resume, progressively bringing portfolio capital flows and foreign direct investment to the region to record levels, exceeding ten times those observed in the previous twenty years (Figure 3.1).

One of the consequences of this process was the deterioration of the region's external current account, which shifted from a balanced position in 1990 to an aggregate deficit of US$ 92 billion in 1998. Foreign direct investment played a major role in explaining the boom in capital inflows, increasing from around US$ 5 billion in 1990 to US$ 55 billion by 1998, to

Figure 3.1. **Latin America: Net inflows of capital, external debt and inflation, 1985-2004**

A. Net capital inflows

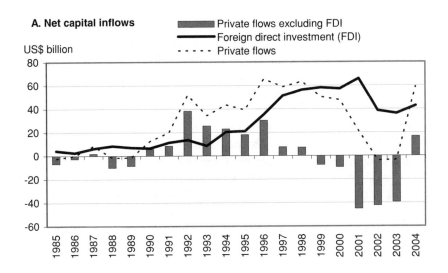

B. External debt and inflation

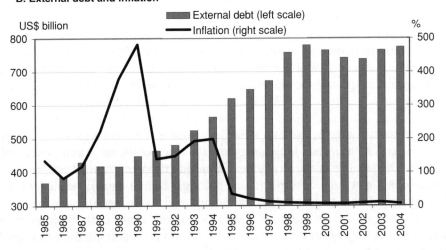

Source: IMF.

subsequently reach a new peak of US$ 65 billion in 2001. Globalisation resulted initially in a marked improvement in macroeconomic performance, as area-wide economic growth reached about 3.5-4.5% per year.

Part of the optimism prevailing in the first half of the 1990s was related to a number of important achievements, particularly disinflation. The tight

CHALLENGES TO FISCAL ADJUSTMENT IN LATIN AMERICA – ISBN 9264022074 © OECD 2006

connection between fiscal largesse and monetary expansion had been at the core of chronic inflation in Latin America during the 1970s and 1980s. Therefore, renewed access by the public sector to international credit allowed central banks in Latin America to become more independent and to focus on fighting inflation and on the development of monetary institutions conducive to price stability. Most countries in the region relied initially on fixed exchange-rate regimes, reflecting the weight placed by policymakers on the objective of building credibility. Similarly, many policymakers encouraged the dollarisation of government debts as a mechanism to break the vicious circle of inflation expectations and fiscal deficits, associated with potentially devastating multiple and self-fulfilling equilibria.[4]

However, the success of Latin American governments at attaining price stability contrasts with their slow progress in improving fiscal performance. The result was that, while inflation collapsed in the region, as well as in emerging market economies in general, external debts rose again as budget deficits took place together with a significant pick-up in private sector indebtedness, fuelled by the recovery in both private investment and consumption. While the yearly rate of inflation dropped from a peak of nearly 500% in 1990 to under 10% by 1998, the region's external debt increased from just above US$ 400 billion in 1989 to over US$ 750 billion in 1998.

The sequence of financial crises that plagued emerging market economies in the second half of the 1990s hit Latin America especially hard after the Russian default in 1998. The external environment that had been benign until then turned extremely volatile. The abundance of capital inflows was followed by a sharp and sudden reduction in the supply of credit to the region and a commensurate increase in risk *premia*, exposing the weaknesses of economic policies. The required adjustment to the new external environment was significant. The region's current account deficit dropped from US$ 92 billion in 1998 to US$ 48 billion in 2000 to finally reach a small surplus of over US$ 4 billion in 2003. This adjustment, however, was significantly lower than in Asia, where current account balances shifted to significant surpluses over a very short period.[5] The adjustment took a toll on economic performance, as the region's rate of growth of output dropped from around 4% in 1998 to just over 1% in 1999, remaining barely positive in 2002. Moreover, as several economies were forced to abandon rigid exchange-rate regimes, the presence of liability dollarisation, both of public debts and in the financial system, became a major source of concern.

The adjustment process induced by the significant reduction in capital flows reflected the unwillingness of lenders to continue to finance private and public borrowing, which was no longer considered sustainable under the new market conditions. However, this new and less favourable external environment did not affect the public and private sectors in the same manner: the brunt of the adjustment was borne by the private sector, as evidenced by a significant improvement in the region's current account balance, while public sector debts and deficits remained high.

One of the reasons why the public sector did not adjust in the same manner as the private sector was that, put simply, many policymakers wanted to prevent fiscal pro-cyclicality in a recession. This line of reasoning was grounded, on the one hand, on conventional optimal (tax smoothing) fiscal policy principles and, on the other, on the belief that international capital markets would (or should!) regard the resulting deficits and debts as sustainable. Such state of affairs reflected the fact that, although IMF conditionality generally recommended reducing budget deficits in order to strengthen fiscal solvency, the conventional fiscal policy framework used by the Fund (and by capital markets) lacked a clear guidance on which debt levels should be viewed as sustainable and which should not. In addition, the higher risk *premia* placed by lenders on the region and the lower capital inflows resulted in a significant decline in investment. This decline – observed in almost all Latin American economies in the aftermath of the Russian crisis – raised concern about potential growth, and hence the sustainability of public indebtedness, in many countries.

Thus, one of the most important lessons of the 1990s is that defining fiscal sustainability is a significantly more complex task than would be suggested by just considering simple definitions of inter-temporal solvency. In particular, this is because, as opposed to industrial countries, emerging market economies have faced significant volatility in capital markets in recent years, often reflecting contagion from other economies with seemingly little connection with the country affected.[6] In this context, the definition of fiscal sustainability becomes particularly difficult, as solvency and liquidity considerations are intertwined. Moreover, sudden stops in financing flows often force fiscal policy to behave pro-cyclically, in contradiction to Barro's (1979) optimal "tax smoothing". In the conventional model, the guiding principle of optimal fiscal policy is the attainment of inter-temporal solvency. By ensuring that the streams of current and future revenue are consistent with current and future outlays in net present value terms, the capital market is assumed to be able to finance temporary deficits motivated by tax smoothing. In this model, any non-increasing debt level is sustainable by definition.

Guidotti (2004) develops the following simple model to illustrate how the concept of fiscal sustainability can be modified if liquidity considerations are taken into account. The evolution over time of the ratio of public debt to GDP, b, is given by:

$$\dot{b} \equiv d - nb, \tag{1}$$

where d denotes the budget deficit as a share of GDP and n is the rate of growth of GDP over the long term. Similarly, the yearly borrowing requirement (net of any pre-funding) as a proportion of GDP, x, can be defined as follows:

$$x \equiv d + \frac{b}{m} \tag{2}$$

where m denotes the average maturity of public debt.[7] Equation (2) simply states that the yearly borrowing requirement is the sum of the deficit plus amortisations.

Given the above definitions, it is useful to obtain an enhanced measure of sustainability where fiscal policy, in addition to being consistent with inter-temporal solvency, also satisfies a liquidity constraint setting a maximum yearly borrowing requirement, x_0. The maximum size of the yearly financial programme is used by market participants to form views on the sustainability of a country's economic policies. Thus, fiscal policy is sustainable when it satisfies Equation (2), where $x = x_0$, and the following relationship between long-run growth and the budget deficit, implying that b is held constant over time:[8]

$$d = nb \tag{3}$$

As a result, the following relationship between sustainable debt and average maturity emerges:

$$b \leq b_{max} \equiv x_0 \frac{m}{1 + nm}. \tag{4}$$

For given x_0 and n, Equation (4) provides a fiscal sustainability criterion that relates a public debt objective (or ceiling) to the maturity structure of public debt.[9] In particular, in order to ensure that a country has an adequate liquidity position with respect to the capital markets, as measured by the yearly borrowing requirement, there is an inverse relationship between average debt maturity, on the one hand, and the sustainable ratios of the budget deficit and long-run debt to GDP, on the other. By Equation (4), the shorter the maturity of the public debt, the tighter the debt ceiling.

Hence, when the conventional tax-smoothing model is modified to account for liquidity constraints in the form of a maximum allowable financing programme, it introduces a stricter condition for debt sustainability. These findings are very much in line with what Reinhart, Rogoff and Savastano (2003) have called "debt intolerance". Interestingly, the "safe" debt ceilings suggested by their study are below 35% of GDP.

The same framework also illustrates a very common dilemma faced by many Latin American economies in recent financial crises, when fiscal policy was required to behave pro-cyclically in response to deteriorating external conditions. Consider an economy that faces a deterioration in market confidence, shown in our model by a reduction in the maximum allowable financing programme, x_0. The hardening of the liquidity constraint, as a sudden stop in capital inflows, is associated with a reduction in the sustainable debt ceiling for a given maturity structure. Guidotti (2004) shows that in order to restore a sustainable fiscal position consistent with the new liquidity constraint, a fiscal adjustment becomes imperative, requiring a sharp increase in the primary budget balance. Over time, as the debt-to-GDP ratio converges to the new long-run equilibrium, the required primary balance is lowered on account of the lower interest bill. These dynamics contrast sharply with the type of response one would predict in a conventional tax-smoothing model. This is because in the present case the shock comes precisely from the capital market, such that fiscal policy is forced to behave pro-cyclically.

In sum, this section illustrates that capital market volatility and sudden stops effectively lead to the emergence of natural debt ceilings, which, when exceeded, may exacerbate country risk and call for pro-cyclical adjustment. These debt ceilings may be more or less stringent depending on the budget's financing needs. In particular, the analysis shows that governments should strive to lengthen the maturity structure of public debt. However, experience also shows that, when governments in emerging markets attempt to develop long-term debt markets, they often resort to issuing debt denominated in foreign currency, as the issuance of long-term domestic currency-denominated debt is often undermined by the weak credibility of their monetary policy.

Re-examining Argentina's fiscal policy in the 1990s

Brady bonds and BOCONes

In light of the considerations made in the previous section on the interaction between capital market behaviour, policy choices and debt sustainability, Argentina's Convertibility regime, established in March 1991,

CHALLENGES TO FISCAL ADJUSTMENT IN LATIN AMERICA – ISBN 9264022074 © OECD 2006

stands out as a particularly extreme example of policy pre-commitment. In addition to adopting a fixed peg to the US dollar in a quasi currency-board arrangement, Convertibility favoured dollarisation by prohibiting all forms of price indexation and by allowing the US dollar to be legal tender for contracts denominated in that currency.[10]

In this context, Argentina's fiscal policy faced significant challenges. In particular, three crucial policy decisions significantly affected the dynamics of public indebtedness in the 1990s. The first two decisions were the signing of the Brady deal, which allowed Argentina to end a protracted period of default, and the recognition by the government of arrears with pensioners and suppliers, which resulted in the issuance of a second type of bonds (BOCONes or *Bonos de Consolidación*) known as "skeletons". Both the Brady bonds and the BOCONes had in common the characteristic of being involuntarily-placed debt, of long duration and low coupons. As a result, a significant portion of Argentina's public debt at the beginning of the 1990s had been issued in favourable terms. Brady bonds and BOCONes accounted for over 25% of the debt stock in 1993. Debt with multilateral organisations accounted for another 16% of public debt, so that over 40% of public debt had been contracted at below-market interest rates. As a result, debt sustainability analysis tended to underestimate the interest bill over the long term.

As the maturing debt had to be rolled over at market rates, the share of involuntary-placed debt in total public debt declined from over 25% in 1993 to about 5% in 2001 (Figure 3.2), and interest payments ballooned from under US$ 3 billion in 1993 to over US$ 10 billion in 2001. In addition to putting significant strain on the fiscal accounts, the flow of debt issued as BOCONes reflected the issuance of court rulings and, as a result, its potential amount was unknown, although these liabilities were recognised on a yearly basis by Congress through the budget. Moreover, because they reflected the consolidation of past arrears, BOCONes were not treated by the government as new debt and, hence, were not recorded above the line.

The issuance of BOCONes had a significant impact on the debt dynamics during Convertibility. While below-the-line calculations show that public debt increased on average by almost 3% of GDP per year during 1993-2000, the above-the-line statistics point to an average budget deficit of only 1% of GDP over the period. Interestingly, the issuance of BOCONes explains over 40% of the increase in the public debt during 1993-2000, on average 1.3% of GDP per year. In summary, the conclusion of the Brady debt restructuring process at the end of 1992 and the government's decision to securitise past arrears affected both future fiscal flows, because interest payments rose as maturing debt was rolled over at market interest rates, as well as the stock of public debt through the continued issuance of BOCONes.

Figure 3.2. **Brady and BOCONes: Restructured debt and the dynamics of interest payments**

A.Brady and BOCONes

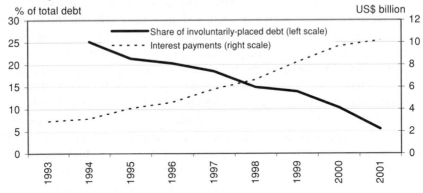

B. Decomposition of public indebtness

Increase in public debt (1993-2000): US$ 64.1 billion

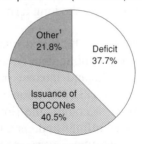

C. Accounting of the pension reform

Increase in public debt (1993-2000): US$ 64.1 billion

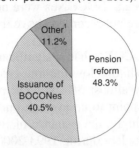

1.   Includes stock valuation changes reflecting exchange rate variations, which are typically accounted for below the line.
Source: Ministry of Economy.

CHALLENGES TO FISCAL ADJUSTMENT IN LATIN AMERICA – ISBN 9264022074 © OECD 2006

Pension reform

In 1993, although the impact of the BOCONes and Brady bonds on the debt dynamics had not been fully evident, a third major decision – the pension reform – was taken. Inspired by the experience of Chile, the reform of Argentina's pension system consisted of replacing the publicly-funded, pay-as-you-go system by a fully-funded one. Although the merits of the pension reform are significant in terms of eliminating a chronic source of fiscal mismanagement and improving the quality of social security, a comprehensive evaluation of the costs and benefits of the reform lies beyond the scope of this chapter. Rather, the analysis will focus on the narrower issue of how the pension reform affected present and future fiscal policy.

From a fiscal point of view, the pension reform implied that employees and employers would start contributing the share of their salary that was financing the pay-as-you-go system into an individual account held by private pension funds. Thus, during a transition period, government revenue would fall by the amount of employees' and employers' contributions to the new system while, at the same time, the government would still continue to pay social security benefits to the current generation of pensioners. As a result, it was clear that the privatisation of the pension system, while contributing to a structural improvement in the public finances in an inter-temporal sense, would generate a transitional deficit. In order to mitigate in part the impact of the reform on the fiscal accounts, the pension funds were forced to invest up to one-half of their assets in government bonds. Simulations suggest that, in the absence of the loss of revenue generated by the reform, the primary balance would have been in surplus during 1993-2000, with the exception of 1996, because of the Tequila crisis, in the range of 2-2.5% of GDP (Figure 3.3). This is against the actual primary surpluses ranging between 0.5-1.0% of GDP per year over the period.

As a result of the ensuing deterioration of the primary balance, the pension reform affected the public debt dynamics. Given that additional debt had to be issued in order to finance the loss of social security revenue, the interest bill also increased. As a result, while the actual debt ratio increased during Convertibility from just above 29% of GDP in 1993 to 54% of GDP in the crisis year of 2001, in the absence of the pension reform the ratio would have risen to about 40% of GDP in 2001 instead. It is important to keep in mind that the drop in output associated with the crisis also affected the debt ratios.

In view of the volatility experienced by emerging markets in the second half of the 1990s, the pension reform may have contributed heavily to the deterioration of investors' perception of Argentina's debt sustainability towards

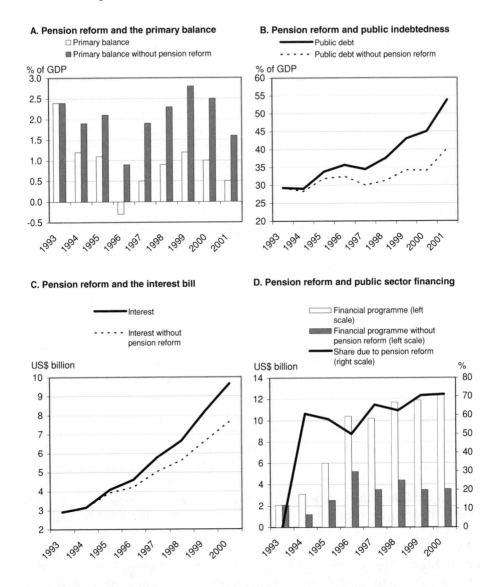

Figure 3.3. **Pension reform and public finances, 1993-2000**

A. Pension reform and the primary balance
□ Primary balance
■ Primary balance without pension reform

% of GDP

B. Pension reform and public indebtedness
━━ Public debt
- - - - Public debt without pension reform

% of GDP

C. Pension reform and the interest bill
━━ Interest
- - - - Interest without pension reform

US$ billion

D. Pension reform and public sector financing
☐ Financial programme (left scale)
■ Financial programme without pension reform (left scale)
━━ Share due to pension reform (right scale)

US$ billion

Source: Ministry of Economy.

the end of the decade. This deterioration was due to the increase not only in the debt-to-GDP ratio but also in the government's borrowing requirements, so that debt sustainability and liquidity considerations were interdependent, as discussed above. While the impact of pension reform on the debt-to-GDP ratio was very significant, that on the actual borrowing requirement was even

CHALLENGES TO FISCAL ADJUSTMENT IN LATIN AMERICA – ISBN 9264022074 © OECD 2006

stronger, rising from a level of US$ 2.1 billion in 1993 to US$ 12.4 billion in 2000, while in the absence of the pension reform it would have increased only to US$ 3.6 billion. The pension reform accounted for over 70% of Argentina's borrowing needs at the end of the 1990s.

These findings are particularly important when attempting to understand the causes of Argentina's recent crisis. In particular, the analysis shows the importance of liquidity considerations when evaluating a country's debt sustainability. If one considers the privatisation of the social security system to have been an important structural reform, ultimately leading to an improvement in public sector solvency, then the market should have financed the transitional medium-term deficit. This was precisely the view held by many supporters of privatisation. However, Argentina's experience shows that liquidity considerations also matter. A debt-to-GDP ratio of 34% and a borrowing requirement of US$ 3.6 billion would hardly have been considered unsustainable by the market in 2000, while a debt-to-GDP ratio of 45% and a borrowing requirement of US$ 12.4 billion certainly were, as the subsequent year's crisis clearly demonstrated. The effects of the pension reform on the dynamics of Argentina's fiscal accounts would have been massive by themselves, but they compounded the effects of the Brady restructuring and the issuance of BOCONes (see also Figure 3.2).

Of the US$ 64.1 billion increase in public debt in the period 1993-2000, a share of about 48% is accounted for by the pension reform—a contribution to the overall average annual budget deficit of 1.6% of GDP. Thus, assuming an unchanged fiscal policy stance, the pension reform and the recognition of skeletons combined explain almost all of the increase in Argentina's public debt during 1993-2000. In light of these findings, the pension reform of 1993 can be considered as a large fiscal bet, taken when external financing conditions were favourable for emerging market economies and when the importance of liquidity considerations and sudden stops in capital flows was not well understood. Given those initial risky policy decisions, the relevant question becomes that of whether or not fiscal policy, which has so far been assumed unchanged, would have responded to the subsequent challenges posed by those policy decisions.

Examining the fiscal policy response

Faced with the challenge of managing the debt dynamics imposed by Brady restructuring, the consolidation of arrears through the issuance of BOCONes and pension reform, policymakers had to respond while considering alternative measures that could have been taken, given the menu of instruments at the government's disposal and the exchange-rate regime in place. Fiscal measures were taken in three main areas: expenditure, revenue and public debt management.

Expenditure

Government expenditure accounts for a relatively low share of GDP in Argentina: less than 25% (Figure 3.4). But a significant portion of primary (non-interest) expenditure is not discretionary, being mandated by the Constitution or specific legislation. In 2000, non-discretionary expenditure, made up largely of pensions and mandatory revenue sharing with the provinces (*Coparticipación*), accounted for about 78% of non-interest expenditure and two-thirds of total spending.[11] Expenditure rigidity is important, as discussed by Lisa Schineller in Chapter 2, because it constrains the options for fiscal adjustment in the absence of exchange rate changes that could alter the value of public sector wages, as in 2002.

Most of the increase in expenditure under Convertibility is explained by an initial increase in non-discretionary spending (from about 11% of GDP in 1993 to about 13% of GDP in 1995) and by the increase in interest payments (from 1.2% of GDP in 1993, or nearly 7% of total expenditure, to 3.4% of GDP in 2000, or over 15% of total expenditure). Within the limitations imposed by its composition, fiscal policy focused on containing discretionary expenditure, especially after 1995. As a result, the ratio of primary spending to GDP remained virtually unchanged during 1995-2000 in the range of 18-19%, and the increase in the interest bill was compensated for by a containment of discretionary expenditure, whose share in total outlays declined from almost 30% in 1993 to over 18% in 2000. In fact, primary expenditure remained frozen in nominal terms after 1997, declining from a level of US$ 53.1 billion in that year to US$ 52.7 billion in 2000.

Revenue

The limitations on fiscal management imposed by the downward rigidity of government expenditure, despite its relatively low level in relation to GDP by international standards, was even more evident when considering the level and composition of revenue. Although effort to improve tax collection was considerable in the 1990s, after inflation had been contained, total tax revenue increased only modestly from 12% of GDP in 1993 to 14% of GDP in 2000. Evasion and poor tax legislation, especially with regard to the income tax, conspired against the government's ability to increase revenue against a background where social security contributions were declining rapidly because of the pension reform and, on the expenditure side, the government was facing an increasingly heavy interest bill.

82

Figure 3.4. **Policy response: Expenditure and revenue decomposition,
1993, 1995, 2000**

A. Expenditure decomposition

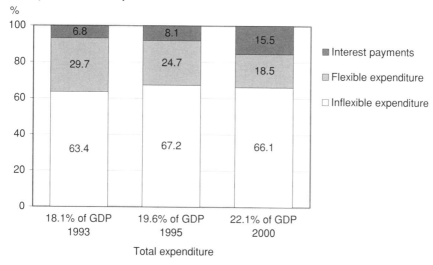

Total expenditure

B. Revenue decomposition

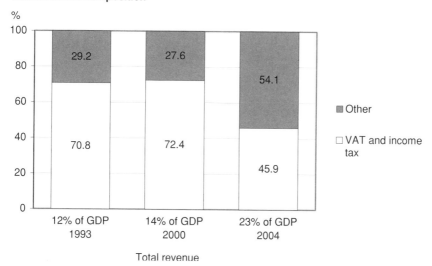

Total revenue

Source: Ministry of Economy.

Despite attempts to boost income tax and VAT collections, which accounted for over 70% of total tax revenue after the reform of the tax code in 1998, the pressure on external competitiveness placed by an appreciating US dollar and falling commodity prices forced the government to use those additional revenues to reduce taxes on payroll. It was only after the collapse of Convertibility and the devaluation of the *peso* that the government was able to raise tax revenue to 23% of GDP, albeit at the cost of imposing two new distorting taxes, on financial transactions and exports, which collect at present around 20% of total tax revenue.

Public debt management

The policy options available in the late 1990s were severely constrained by downward rigidity in expenditure, an inefficient tax system and a rigid exchange-rate regime against the backdrop of deteriorating external competitiveness. Fiscal policymakers were therefore confronted with the challenges of dealing with the dynamics imposed by the Brady deal, the pension reform and the recognition of skeletons when international capital market turned volatile after the Asian crisis and the Russian default. At the same time, as policymakers and investors alike were trying to come to terms with the phenomenon of sudden stops in capital flows to emerging markets, Argentina's government made significant effort to improve its budget financing strategy (Figure 3.5).

As financing needs increased, the government aimed at improving the composition of public debt. In particular, especially starting in 1996, the maturity of new issues rose from 3 years in 1993 to almost 11 years in 1998,

Figure 3.5. **Policy response: Debt management, 1993-2000**

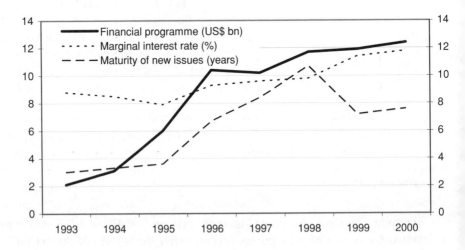

Source: Ministry of Economy.

CHALLENGES TO FISCAL ADJUSTMENT IN LATIN AMERICA – ISBN 9264022074 © OECD 2006

only to drop because of adverse market conditions again in 1999 to just over 7 years. The policy of increasing the maturity of public debt was complemented by that of building a liquidity cushion at the Treasury to cover financing needs 3 months in advance.[12] While these policies initially reassured lenders, they resulted in an increase in the interest bill. The interest rate paid on new debt issues increased from about 8% in 1995 to almost 12% in 2000, reflecting capital market volatility.

Conclusions and final considerations

Argentina's experience is illustrative of the potentially complex elements that affect a country's debt sustainability when liquidity considerations play a crucial role in shaping investors' behaviour. It also shows the importance of understanding the dynamic effects that important policy decisions, such as debt restructuring or the privatisation of social security, have on the fiscal accounts over time in light of the existing policy instruments and borrowing restrictions.

This paper argues against the conventional view that fiscal policy was irresponsible during the 1990s and that the consequent build-up of public debt was at the heart of the 2001 crisis. To this end, I have shown that fiscal policymaking was responsible within the limitations of the available instruments and the restrictions placed by the exchange-rate regime in place. What created a seemingly unsustainable debt dynamics was the implementation of a highly acclaimed reform of the pension system in a context where the country's public finances were already under considerable stress due to the Brady deal and the recognition of *skeletons*. I say seemingly because, at the time when the pension reform was implemented, it was not thought to be inconsistent with prudent fiscal policy in the sense that, as the reform would improve public sector solvency in an inter-temporal sense, it should have been financed by the market. But, of course, it wasn't. While policy was framed in the conventional tax-smoothing framework, reality showed that liquidity constraints and sudden stops finally determined what was feasible and what was not.

This lesson is very important also when analysing the role of IMF financing, especially in light of the fact that many Latin American economies have followed the path of Chile in privatising their social security system, without having put in place the fiscal instruments to finance the transition costs imposed by the reform. A better understanding of the role of optimal debt ceilings should help prevent the adoption of desirable, but eventually unsustainable reforms, when liquidity considerations and the availability of official financing to mitigate the dynamic effects of costly structural reforms are taken into account.

The analysis also has important implications for debt restructuring. In particular, the Brady deal, as well as other more recent arrangements, show that public debt restructuring often leaves the debtor country with a "debt overhang" that is not incorporated in the design of fiscal policy, leading to what Reinhart, Rogoff and Savastano (2003) have called "serial default". At the time of debt restructuring, preference is often given to the idea that capital is rolled over the long term (preferably with limited haircut) so that new bonds are typically issued with long maturities, low coupons and long initial grace periods in order to alleviate the country's borrowing requirement in the initial phase of return to market financing. Long maturities and low coupons, coupled with a high discount rate, give the impression that the restructuring debtor has obtained a significant net present value haircut. Of course, the problems materialise at a later stage, as the roll-over of these obligations has to be undertaken in significantly worse market conditions, inducing an increase in interest payments that may not be politically palatable.

The problem can be illustrated by comparing debt restructurings in the private and public sectors. When a private company is forced to restructure its obligations the important variable that creditors and the debtor look at is how debt reduction affects the value of the firm. Hence, in the absence of liquidity considerations, the relevant variable in restructuring is the debt reduction in net present value terms. The structure of the new debt (*i.e.* its maturity and coupon) is irrelevant so long as it yields a given net present value reduction. As the firm maximises profits, and hence value, it is well known that the structure of the new debt matters only to the extent that liquidity considerations are important.

On the contrary, when the public sector restructures its debt, the structure of the new debt may matter even in the absence of liquidity considerations. The reason is that governments and the political establishment tend to have a shorter horizon than that used in the net present value calculations. Hence, a restructuring that carries low coupons and long grace periods will tend to induce the government to carry out a relatively lax fiscal policy relative to the situation in which it has to face interest payments based on market rates from the beginning. When fiscal adjustment is needed at a later stage, as the new debt matures and has to be rolled over at market rates, political support tends to be more difficult to secure. In sum, the criteria used in private debt restructurings may not be applicable directly to sovereign debt restructurings. For the sake of fiscal transparency and to avoid future debt overhangs, the latter should favour the use of discount bonds, carrying an outright capital haircut, and coupons which reflect market interest rates.

CHALLENGES TO FISCAL ADJUSTMENT IN LATIN AMERICA – ISBN 9264022074 © OECD 2006

Comments

Oscar Cetrángolo,

ECLAC, Buenos Aires Office

Introduction

Pablo Guidotti's chapter focuses on global finances and offers a very thorough and motivating view of Argentina's fiscal policy in the 1990s from a macroeconomic perspective. My intention is to complement his analysis – although it does not mean that I endorse it – with more public finance-oriented remarks. I will refer to fiscal adjustment during the 1990s by beginning to place it in a historical perspective, describing the post-crisis developments and discussing a few challenges ahead.[13]

Fiscal adjustment during the 1990s from a historical perspective

The conventional views of Argentina's crisis are concentrated on the fiscal problems the country faced during the 1990s. There is abundant information on the deterioration of Argentina's fiscal accounts over the period and the absence of fiscal adjustment. However, long-term series suggest that the 1990s were a period of impressive adjustment in comparison with the previous decades (Table 3.1), even if privatisation revenue is taken into account. During the three previous decades, the Argentine public sector had posted primary deficits exceeding 4% of GDP, which were largely associated with the loss of inflation-tax revenue. Thus, the fiscal problems of the 1990s did not arise from a lack of fiscal adjustment, but from the inconsistency between fiscal policy and the macroeconomic regime.

The fiscal stress of the 1990s was primarily related to three factors. Without any doubt, I agree with Pablo Guidotti that pension reform has seriously affected the primary balance and will continue to do so for a long time. Although the social security reform of 1994 was necessary, it was not consistent with the need for fiscal consolidation. The second factor was, indeed, the poor performance of tax collection. This was due in part to the need to eliminate the taxes that had an adverse impact on competitiveness. Finally, the provinces' fiscal problems were particularly acute in the mid-1990s, after the Tequila crisis.

Post-crisis adjustment

Fiscal adjustment after the crisis was impressive. The main factors leading to the strengthening of public finances, in addition to the debt default itself, with no direct implication for the primary balance, are related to a very special relative-price configuration. Contributing factors include the reduction in real wages, mainly for civil servants, and social security benefits, coupled with the taxation of exports after the abandonment of Convertibility. The reduction in real wages at the central government level resulted in savings of almost 0.5% of GDP and 1% of GDP in pensions during 2001-03. At the same time, tax revenue from exports reached 2.5% of GDP in 2003. In sum, this period could be characterised as one of "relative-price fiscal adjustment".

The challenges ahead

I will focus on four main challenges associated with the recovery of the Argentine economy after the crisis and default, which are related to the long-run sustainability of public finances after debt restructuring. They are: tax reform, the pension system, intergovernmental relations and spending on social protection.

Table 3.1. **Fiscal outcomes, 1961-2003**
Headline budget balance in per cent of GDP
(National non-financial public sector, accrual basis, period averages)

	Headline balance		Primary balance	
	With privatisation revenue	Without privatisation revenue	With privatisation revenue	Without privatisation revenue
1961-70	-3.5	-3.5	-2.9	-2.9
1971-80	-6.7	-6.7	-5.7	-5.7
1981-90	-6.2	-6.2	-4.4	-4.4
1991-2001	-1.5	-1.8	0.6	0.2
2002-03	0.6	0.6	2.6	2.6
1961-90	-5.5	-5.5	-4.3	-4.3
1961-2003	-4.2	-4.3	-2.7	-2.9

Source: Cetrángolo and Jiménez (2003).

CHALLENGES TO FISCAL ADJUSTMENT IN LATIN AMERICA – ISBN 9264022074 © OECD 2006

First, Argentina reached its highest tax ratio in 2004, at around 26.5% of GDP. This was due to the taxation of exports and the introduction of extraordinary tax measures which, jointly, accounted for almost 17% of the tax burden. The main challenge, therefore, is to replace these temporary measures by traditional and permanent sources of revenue. In this sense, the ultimate policy goal is to maintain the present tax burden through improvements in the administration of traditional taxes, which depends on the extension of the transition period and the evolution of relative prices.

Second, much effort has been made to reform the revenue-sharing arrangements across the different levels of government. The instability of the tax system is a complicating factor, making it hard to achieve the needed consensus for further reform in this area. Instead, it is more important to consolidate the fiscal position of the sub-national governments, ensuring its sustainability over the longer term, and to pursue structural reform aimed at improving the efficiency of education, health care and other public services.

Third, there is an urgent need for further pension reform. Pablo Guidotti places the pension reform of the early 1990s at the core of Argentina's fiscal stress. I will not to delve deeply into this issue, but it is important to note that, in addition to the fiscal pressure arising from the transition costs generated by the reform, problems remain in the design of the new system. Problems also arose from Convertibility itself as the government had to reduce the tax burden on labour as a means of boosting competitiveness. In addition, the coverage of social security is low, with 35% of the population aged 65 years or more having no pension protection and only 36% of the economically active population now contributing to a pension fund. This calls for an adequate combination of a public pay-as-you-go system, a private capitalisation scheme and a publicly-funded social protection programme for the elderly without coverage.

Finally, and related to the issue of long-term sustainability, future budgeting in Argentina has to take note of new problems associated with the increase in unemployment, rising informality in the labour market (*i.e.* no social security coverage) and mounting pressure on the public health care and education systems, among others. In sum, an increasing portion of public expenditure will need to be redirected to new social protection programmes.

Notes

1.   Calvo, Izquierdo and Talvi (2002), in particular, emphasise the role of the exchange-rate regime in view of significant necessary changes in relative

prices as well as the role of liability dollarisation and the associated balance-sheet effects in explaining the 2001 crisis.

2.   See IMF's Independent Evaluation Office (2004) on the role of the IMF in Argentina.

3.   This section is based on Guidotti (2004).

4.   The relationship between liability dollarisation and the credibility of a monetary/exchange-rate anchor has been explored in the literature. See, for instance, Calvo (1989) and Calvo and Guidotti (1990).

5.   See, for instance, Calvo, Izquierdo and Mejía (2003), Calvo and Talvi (2003) and Guidotti, Sturzenegger, and Villar (2004).

6.   See Calvo (2002) for further discussion on financial contagion.

7.   It is assumed, for simplicity, that amortisations are uniformly distributed over time.

8.   Equation (2) would hold with an inequality in the presence of debt aversion, as defined by Calvo and Guidotti (1992).

9.   If, for instance, the maximum allowable yearly financing programme equals 7% of GDP, the growth rate equals 3.5%, and the average maturity of the public debt equals 5 years, then Equation (4) implies a debt ceiling of 30% of GDP. If, in the same example, average maturity declines to 3 (increases to 7) years, then the corresponding debt ceiling declines to 19% (increases to 40%) of GDP.

10.   The Convertibility regime was a quasi currency-board arrangement because, although it required international reserves to be at least equal to base money at all times, a portion of those reserves could be held in the form of dollar-denominated government bonds.

11.   Payroll is not considered non-discretionary expenditure. Discretionary expenditures include wages, outlays in goods and services, and public investment.

12.   See Guidotti (2003) for a more detailed discussion of public debt management strategies.

13.   Many of the views presented here have been presented more thoroughly elsewhere; in particular, in Cetrángolo and Jimenez (2003, 2004) and Cetrángolo and Grushka (2004).

CHALLENGES TO FISCAL ADJUSTMENT IN LATIN AMERICA – ISBN 9264022074 © OECD 2006

Bibliography

Barro, R. (1979), "On the Determination of the Public Debt", *Journal of Political Economy*, Vol. 87, No. 5, pp. 940-71.

Calvo, G. (1989), "Incredible Reforms", in G. Calvo, R. Findlay, P. Kouri and J. Braga de Macedo (eds), *Debt, Stabilization and Development*, Basil Blackwell.

Calvo, G. (2002), "Contagion in Emerging Markets: When Wall Street is a Carrier", in *Proceedings from the International Economic Association Congress*, Vol. 3. Buenos Aires.

Calvo, G. and P.E. Guidotti (1990), "Indexation and Maturity of Government Bonds: An Exploratory Model", in R. Dornbusch and M. Draghi (eds.), *Public Debt Management·Theory and History*, Cambridge University Press, Cambridge.

Calvo, G. and P.E. Guidotti (1992), "Optimal Maturity of Nominal Government Debt: An Infinite-Horizon Model", *International Economic Review*, Vol. 33, pp. 895-919.

Calvo, G., A. Izquierdo and L.F. Mejía (2003), "On the Empirics of Sudden Stops", *Working Paper*, Inter-American Development Bank, Washington, D.C.

Calvo, G., A. Izquierdo and E. Talvi (2002), "Sudden Stops, the Real Exchange Rate, and Fiscal Sustainability: Argentina's Lessons", *Working Paper*, Inter-American Development Bank, Washington, D.C.

Calvo, G. and E. Talvi (2003), *Latin Macro Watch*, Inter-American Development Bank, Washington, D.C.

Cetrángolo, O. and J.P. Jiménez (2003), "Política Fiscal en Argentina Durante el Régimen de Convertibilidad", *Serie Gestión Pública*, No. 25, ILPES-ECLAC, Santiago.

Cetrángolo, O. and J.P. Jiménez (2004), "Las Relaciones entre Niveles de Gobierno en Argentina", *Revista de la CEPAL*, No. 84, pp. 117-34.

Cetrángolo, O. and C. Grushka (2004), "Sistema Previsional Argentino: Crisis, Reforma y Crisis de la Reforma", *Serie Financiamiento del Desarrollo*, No. 151, ECLAC, Santiago.

Guidotti, P. E. (2003), "Toward a Liquidity Risk Management Strategy for Emerging Market Economies", in J. Gonzalez, V. Corbo, A. Krueger and A. Tornell (eds.) *Latin American Macroeconomic Reforms: The Second Stage*, The University of Chicago Press, Chicago, IL.

Guidotti, P.E. (2004), "Global Finance, Macroeconomic Performance, and Policy Response in Latin America: Lessons from the 1990s", *Working Paper*, Universidad Torcuato di Tella, Buenos Aires.

Guidotti, P.E., F Sturzenegger and A. Villar (2004), "On the Consequences of Sudden Stops", *Economia*, Vol. 4, No. 2, pp. 171-214.

International Monetary Fund's Independent Evaluation Office (2004), *Evaluation of the Role of the IMF in Argentina, 1991-2001*, IMF's Independent Evaluation Office ,Washington, D.C.

Mussa, M. (2002), "Argentina and the Fund: From Triumph to Tragedy", *Policy Analyses in International Economics*, No. 67, Institute for International Economics, Washington, D.C.

Perry, G. and L. Servén (2003), "The Anatomy of a Multiple Crisis: Why Was Argentina Special and What We Can Learn From It?", *World Bank Working Paper*, No. 3081, The World Bank, Washington, D.C.

Reinhart, C.M., K.S. Rogoff and M.A. Savastano (2003), "Debt Intolerance", *NBER Working Paper*, No. 9908, NBER, Cambridge, MA.

Chapter 4

The Brazilian fiscal adjustment: Structural change and policy continuity, 1995–2004

Fabio Giambiagi   and   Marcio Ronci*

IPEA   IMF

This chapter discusses fiscal adjustment in Brazil since macroeconomic stabilisation in the mid-1990s. It is argued that the authorities' growing awareness of the need for fiscal discipline was as important as the pace of structural reforms for understanding the dynamics of public indebtedness. Fiscal adjustment intensified after the abandonment of the exchange rate peg in 1999 to avoid a default on the public debt with certainly ruinous consequences for the economy. The chapter discusses the composition of fiscal adjustment, based predominantly on tax revenue hikes, against the backdrop of Brazil's still high public debt-to-GDP ratio, and concludes that the hard-won fiscal discipline will have to be entrenched in fiscal institutions and the quality of the fiscal adjustment improved to support higher and sustainable economic growth.

*   The authors wish to thank Murilo Portugal and David Edwin Wynn Owen for comments. The views expressed in this chapter are those of the authors only, and do not necessarily represent those of the Brazilian government or the International Monetary Fund.

Introduction

After the *Real* Plan of June 1994, Brazil adopted an impressive series of structural and institutional reforms during the two Fernando Henrique Cardoso administrations (1995-98 and 1999-2002) and the current Luiz Inácio "Lula" da Silva administration (2003-06). These reforms are reflected in a notable fiscal adjustment after 1999. The change in the authorities' attitude to fiscal austerity, compared with the pre-1999 expenditure-driven stance, has been remarkable, as well as the continuity of the thrust of the structural and institutional reforms implemented during 1995-2004. The political parties now have a reasonable degree of agreement (not unanimity) on the need for fiscal austerity.

This chapter briefly reviews the main structural and institutional reforms implemented during 1995-2004, the fiscal adjustment that took place after 1999 and the main challenges for the future in terms of fiscal sustainability. Our main conclusion is that, after a decade of structural and fiscal adjustment, there is still a need to consolidate the progress achieved so far by building solid fiscal institutions and improving the quality of fiscal adjustment in support of higher, sustainable economic growth.

The Cardoso and Lula administrations

The first Cardoso administration (1995-98): From stabilisation to structural reform[1]

The first structural reform of the Cardoso administration was the stabilisation of prices. Before price stability was achieved, budgets used to be approved in nominal terms against a backdrop of high and variable inflation. Once the "veil" of inflation was lifted and the inflation tax eliminated, it became clear that rising expenditure would have to be financed by increasing taxes and/or public debt. For the first time in more than 20 years, the Brazilian society was faced with the costs of increasing expenditure in real terms. In support of stabilisation, the authorities implemented a far-reaching series of institutional and structural reforms including the refinancing of state government debts, the (partial) social security reform, the phasing-out of state monopolies, the privatisation of public enterprises and the restructuring of the financial sector.

In the first Cardoso administration, there was an effort to strengthen state and municipal finances. The federal government refinanced state and municipal government debts for a period of over 30 years through legally-binding, bilateral agreements.[2] The refinancing of these sub-national debts was collateralised with future state and municipal revenue, which prompted the sub-national governments to implement fiscal adjustment programmes to repay their debts to the federal government. Also, the social security system underwent important reforms. A constitutional amendment was approved in 1998 increasing the retirement age for newly-hired public-sector workers to 60 years for men and 55 years for women, and changing the calculation of pension benefits for private-sector workers. These workers had their pension benefits reduced according to their retirement age, which created an incentive for postponing retirement.[3]

One of the most remarkable achievements of the first Cardoso administration was the end of state monopolies in telecommunications and oil. These state monopolies posed a structural problem because of the large investments needed in both sectors and the budget constraints facing the public sector. The opening of the oil and telecommunications sectors to competition resulted in a boom of investment. The privatisation of public enterprises also represented a significant structural change. In addition to raising more than US$ 100 billion in proceeds in the 1990s, privatisation removed a potential source of pressure on government spending. Loss-making state-owned companies were sold and the profitable ones were faced with harder budget constraints. The result was an improvement in the primary balance of the state-owned enterprises and an increase in the level of investment in key sectors of the economy.

Finally, a programme was implemented during the 1990s to strengthen the financial system, therefore removing a source of contingent liabilities for the budget. While countries such as Venezuela, with the crisis of *Banco Latino* in the early 1990s, Mexico after the devaluation of 1994 and Argentina in 2001-02 had to bear much higher fiscal costs associated with bank restructuring, Brazil's programme for restructuring and strengthening the national financial system (PROER) allowed the country to weather a sharp exchange rate devaluation in 1999 with limited costs in terms of quasi-fiscal expenditure to support the banks (about 2% of GDP). Also, the federal government privatised most of the state-owned banks, definitely closing a financing window for the state government treasuries.

Despite the 1995-98 reforms, fiscal outcomes were disappointing because of the government's inability to control public expenditure, coupled with the slower-than-expected maturing of the structural reforms, such as privatisation and the control of state and municipal finances. The consolidated public sector primary (excluding interest payments) deficit accounted for 0.2% of GDP on average in 1995-98, while the public sector budget deficit, including interest payments, was about 7% of GDP on average over the same period (Table 4.1).

In particular, central government primary expenditure rose by 7% per year on average during 1995-98, compared with GDP growth of less than 3% per year (Table 4.2).

In this context, the public debt-to-GDP ratio was clearly unsustainable (Figure 4.1). The combination of Brazil's high public external and domestic indebtedness triggered a balance-of-payments crisis in the second half of 1998, eventually leading to the floating of the *real* in January 1999. By the end of

Table 4.1. **Budget balance, 1995-2004**
Consolidated public sector, period averages in per cent of GDP
(a negative number indicates a deficit)

	1995-98	1999-2004
Headline budget balance	-6.7	-4.2
Primary balance	-0.2	3.8
Central government	0.3	2.3
States and municipalities	-0.4	0.7
Public enterprises	-0.1	0.8
Federal	0.2	0.6
State and municipal	-0.2	0.2
Interest payments	6.5	8.1

Source: Central Bank of Brazil.

Table 4.2. **Expenditure growth, 1995-2004**
Central government, period averages in per cent

	1995-98	1999-02	2003	2004
Total primary expenditure[1]	7.1	4.7	-4.2	8.9
Transfers to the states and municipalities	6.8	11.2	-6.7	4.3
Payroll	2.3	4.2	-7.4	4.5
Social security benefits	7.4	5.0	5.8	9.2
Other	13.2	1.1	-11.3	17.0
Memorandum item:				
GDP growth rate	2.6	2.1	0.5	5.2

1. Calculated on the basis of the GDP deflator.
Source: National Treasury.

CHALLENGES TO FISCAL ADJUSTMENT IN LATIN AMERICA – ISBN 9264022074 © OECD 2006

Figure 4.1. **Public indebtedness, 1994-2004**
In per cent of GDP

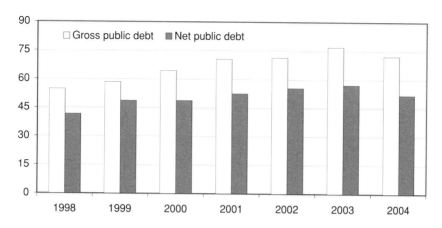

Source: Central Bank of Brazil.

1998, the country signed a Stand-By Arrangement with the International Monetary Fund (IMF) underpinned by a strong fiscal adjustment. The fiscal targets were increased after the devaluation and, as a result, the consolidated primary surplus, which was virtually zero in 1998, rose to over 3% of GDP in 1999.

The second Cardoso administration (1999-2002): Consolidation of structural reform and further fiscal adjustment[4]

In the second Cardoso administration (1999-2002), the consolidated primary budget surplus exceeded the targets set in the IMF programmes, increasing every year as a proportion of GDP. Public finances improved at all levels of government.

The post-1999 fiscal adjustment was related to several factors. The increase in the central government's primary budget surplus was due essentially to a rise in the tax take on the back of an increase in the rates of the taxes on financial transactions (CPMF) and enterprise turnover (COFINS), whose revenue is earmarked for the social security system (Table 4.3). State and municipal primary balances rose substantially as a result of the constraints imposed on their finances by the bilateral debt restructuring arrangements with the federal government and continued compliance with the Fiscal Responsibility Law (FRL). Also, sub-national finances benefited from higher tax revenue on some goods and services that accounted for a large share of the sub-national tax

Table 4.3. **Primary budget surplus, revenue and expenditure, 1995-2004**
Central government, period averages in per cent of GDP

	1995-98	1999-2004
Primary budget surplus	0.3	2.3
Revenue	18.6	22.8
Primary expenditure	18.2	20.6
Payroll	5.2	5.2
Social security benefits	5.4	6.5
Transfers to the states and municipalities	2.8	3.8
Other[1]	4.8	5.1
Statistical discrepancy[2]	0.1	-0.1

1. Includes the primary balance of the Central Bank of Brazil.
2. A positive number indicates an increase in the primary budget surplus.
Source: National Treasury.

base, such as petroleum derivatives, telecommunications and electricity, whose prices rose faster than average after the floating of the *real*. Petrobras, the national oil company and largest state-owned enterprise, posted higher profits because of the increase in international oil prices, given that the company's production covers almost all domestic consumption of petroleum derivatives, while the domestic price of oil tracks international prices closely. The state and municipal enterprises underwent a radical change in their balance sheets after the sale of their loss-making subsidiaries, posting a primary surplus of 0.2% of GDP in 1999-2002, compared with an average primary deficit of 0.2% of GDP during 1995-98.

The approval of the Fiscal Responsibility Law in May 2000 introduced ceilings on government spending on payroll in relation to revenue and prohibited the refinancing of state and municipal debts by the federal government. These provisions put an end to the moral hazard associated with private-sector lending to the state and municipal governments on expectation of a bail-out by the National Treasury. The states and municipalities were faced with a hard-budget constraint for the first time.

However, the most important change after 1999 was the authorities' commitment to fiscal austerity. They considered it difficult to avoid a default on the public debt, with serious consequences for the economy, unless they delivered a substantial primary budget surplus. While expenditure pressures resulted in fiscal imbalances and rising indebtedness before 1999, there has been a clear understanding since then that fiscal adjustment should be achieved

CHALLENGES TO FISCAL ADJUSTMENT IN LATIN AMERICA – ISBN 9264022074 © OECD 2006

through cuts in expenditure and/or increases in revenue. However, despite rising primary surpluses during 1999-2002, the gross public debt continued to increase, reaching over 70% of GDP in 2002. This is because of the increase in interest payments associated with interest- and exchange-rate volatility, given that the public debt is partially indexed to the US dollar and pays floating interest rates, as well as "once-and-for-all" factors, such as the recording of previously unregistered liabilities ("skeletons") (Table 4.4).

The Lula administration: Continuing structural reform and fiscal adjustment

The Lula administration took office in January 2003 under the pressure of rising inflation (12.5% on a year-on-year basis in 2002) and public indebtedness,[5] associated with the impact of the exchange rate depreciation that took place in the run-up to the presidential election in October 2002.[6] The new administration's track record in addressing both problems has so far been good. The monetary authorities reacted swiftly, raising the policy interest rate in early 2003; as a consequence, inflation declined to 9.3% in 2003 and 7.6% in 2004. At the same time, the high real interest rates needed to bring down inflation resulted in an increase in interest payments on the public debt. To keep the debt dynamics sustainable, the authorities announced an increase in the primary surplus target for 2003, which had initially been set at 3.75% of GDP, to 4.25% of GDP. As part of their strategy to restore confidence, the authorities also announced that this higher primary surplus target would be maintained during the remainder of the Lula administration's term in office (2004-06).

Table 4.4. **Composition of net public debt, 1995-2004**
Consolidated public sector, period averages in per cent of GDP

	1995-98	1999-2004	2004
Total net debt[1]	35.0	52.4	51.8
Fiscal debt (excludes stock adjustments)	34.2	39.6	37.9
Stock adjustments	0.8	12.9	13.9
Privatisation receipts	-1.4	-4.2	-3.5
Effect of exchange rate variation on the domestic debt	0.1	6.6	6.8
Effect of exchange rate variation on the external debt	0.2	5.2	5.2
Other[2]	1.8	5.4	5.4

1. Gross public debt less public assets, including international reserves.
2. Recording of previously unregistered debts.
Source: Central Bank of Brazil.

Fiscal performance has been strong. The consolidated public sector recorded a primary budget surplus of 4.3% of GDP in 2003 and 4.6% of GDP in 2004. These positive outcomes resulted from a cut in expenditure in 2003 and an increase in taxes in 2004. The FRL has been preserved, constraining the states and municipalities to maintain a combined primary surplus of about 1% of GDP. Also, the state-owned companies have continued to post primary surpluses.

The thrust of the Cardoso administration's reform efforts was maintained in 2003 with the approval of important pieces of legislation. The tax burden on exports was reduced, but the tax take as a whole rose to over 35% of GDP in 2004. A new social security reform extended personal income taxation to the pension benefits of retired public-sector employees and established a minimum retirement age of 60 years for men and 55 years for women for all public-sector employees.

As a consequence of the combination of good fiscal outturns, further structural reform and an external current account surplus of nearly US$ 12 billion in 2004 (almost 2% of GDP), the country's risk premium fell in 2004 to below its 2002 level, leading to a relaxation of the monetary stance in the second half of the year at no cost to disinflation. In this context, for the first time in 10 years the gross public debt-to-GDP ratio declined to 72% in 2004 from 77% in 2003, while the net external public debt-to-exports ratio fell to 170% in 2004 from about 400% in 1999 (Figure 4.2).

Figure 4.2. **Net external debt, 1981-2004**[1]
In per cent of exports of goods and services

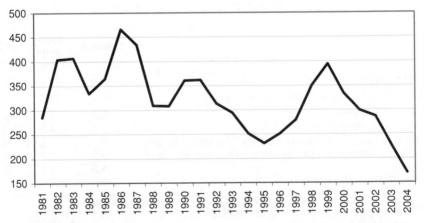

1. External debt less external assets.
Source: Central Bank of Brazil.

CHALLENGES TO FISCAL ADJUSTMENT IN LATIN AMERICA – ISBN 9264022074 © OECD 2006

The future of fiscal sustainability

In this relatively favourable economic environment, what are the most important challenges ahead for Brazil's public finances? After a decade of structural and fiscal adjustment, there is still a need to consolidate the progress achieved so far by strengthening the fiscal institutions and improving the quality of fiscal adjustment in support of higher, sustainable economic growth. Pressure for higher government spending on social programmes is legitimate and likely to intensify in the years ahead. However, the benefits of strengthening fiscal institutions could be large in terms of higher, less unstable growth and enhanced resilience to external shocks. In this regard, the experience of some OECD countries, such as Ireland, Italy and Spain, is instructive. These countries illustrate episodes of successful fiscal adjustment within the European Union institutional framework, having had to maintain primary budget surpluses for extended periods to build credibility and reduce public indebtedness.

In the case of Brazil, five challenges seem to be particularly relevant: entrenching fiscal adjustment, restoring confidence in the public debt, increasing public savings, deepening the social security reforms and reducing the tax burden. Achieving these objectives would create room for reducing interest rates and maintaining low inflation, which would foster investment and growth. At the same time, there is a need to improve the quality of fiscal adjustment by containing public current expenditure, increasing public investment and reducing the tax burden on the private sector.

Entrenching fiscal adjustment through sound institutions

Despite the impressive track record of the last few years, the Brazilian fiscal institutions are still fragile. While the LRF and the refinancing of state and municipal debts introduced a hard-budget constraint at the sub-national levels of government, public finances at the federal level have not been constrained in the same way. The federal government's primary surplus targets are binding only for the current fiscal year and those for the next two years can be revised in the following budget. As such, there is in principle no clear, durable budget constraint at the federal level to prevent a substantial reduction in the primary budget surplus that could lead to increasing debt-to-GDP ratios. Also, it has been exceedingly difficult to curb central government primary expenditure (excluding interest payment), which rose in real terms faster than real GDP during the two Cardoso administrations. Despite the reduction in 2003, primary spending rose by nearly 8.9% in 2004 (Figure 4.3).

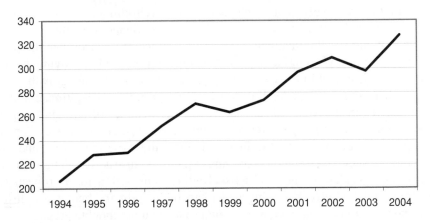

Figure 4.3. **Primary expenditure, 1994-2004**
Central government, in billions of *reais* of 2005[1]

1.   Calculated on the basis of the GDP deflator.
Source: National Treasury.

A possible way to entrench fiscal austerity is to pass a Fiscal Solvency Law complementing the FRL and setting a floor for the primary budget surplus or a ceiling for the budget deficit of the federal government. An alternative approach, perhaps politically more palatable, would be to maintain large primary budget surpluses for many years (leading to a significant decline in the gross debt-to-GDP ratio) so that fiscal austerity is definitely entrenched in society's and the authorities' fiscal attitude.

Restoring the government's creditworthiness

The level of the public debt-to-GDP ratio remains a relevant issue in Brazil, with some observers continuing to put in question its sustainability and the unacceptable burden its financing places on society in terms of sovereign credit risk.[7] While Brazil's public debt is not high in comparison with several OECD countries (Figure 4.4), debt service is comparatively more expensive because rollover risks are perceived as higher. Building trust in the government's commitment to repay its debt is therefore vital for creating an environment of low interest rates and higher economic growth.

Even considering that gradually reducing the gross public debt-to-GDP ratio is a sensible strategy to restore credibility, a more ambitious policy objective should be considered, aiming at reducing the gross public debt-to-GDP ratio to under 50% of GDP in 10 years. The combination of an additional small increase in the primary budget surplus and a gradual decline

CHALLENGES TO FISCAL ADJUSTMENT IN LATIN AMERICA – ISBN 9264022074 © OECD 2006

Figure 4.4. **Gross public debt and primary budget surplus, 1998 and 2004**
In per cent of GDP

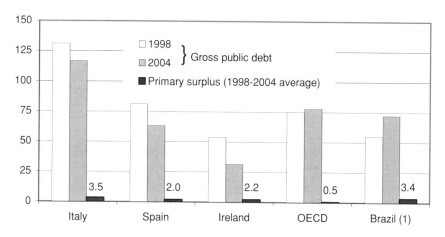

1.   For Brazil, 1998 data were adjusted for hidden liabilities.
Source: Central Bank of Brazil and *OECD Economic Outlook*, No. 76.

of the interest burden, without an offsetting increase in expenditure,[8] would allow the authorities to carry out an aggressive liability management strategy by retiring debt, increasing the average maturity of the debt stock and reducing foreign-exchange exposure, thus allaying concern about the government's ability to service its debt and leading to further reductions in interest rates.[9] An extended period of falling debt-to-GDP ratio would have tremendous implications for reducing country risk and lengthening private investment horizons.

Increasing public saving

Low public saving throughout 1995-2003 contributed to aggravating Brazil's relatively low domestic saving rate (Table 4.5). Maintaining growth rates of more than 4% per year will require a substantial increase in domestic saving, and the government will need to make an effort to reduce its current expenditure to finance more public investment in infrastructure. This change in the composition of government expenditure in favour of capital outlays would deliver a significant improvement in the quality of the fiscal adjustment accomplished so far.

Table 4.5. **Public saving and investment, 1995-2003**
Period averages, in per cent of GDP

	1995-98	1999-2003	2003
Public investment	2.4	1.9	1.5
Domestic saving	16.4	16.0	18.9
Public[1]	-2.1	0.7	-2.1
Private	18.5	15.3	21.0

1. Public saving is defined as public investment minus the operational balance (headline balance minus real interest payment) of the central government and the states and municipalities combined.
Source: Central Bank of Brazil and Brazilian Institute of Geography and Statistics (IBGE).

Deepening the social security reforms

Despite the reforms implemented by the Cardoso and Lula administrations, social security entitlements continue to be relatively generous from an international perspective, putting upward pressure on government expenditure (Figure 4.5). Most pensioners have benefited from real increases in their pension benefits because the minimum pension is indexed to the minimum wage, which increased by nearly 60% in real terms during 1995-2004. Also, 60% of new pensioners have less than 55 years of age (Table 4.6) and entitlements for females are overly generous.[10] Consequently, containing social security expenditure by curbing the increase in the value of benefits is a necessary condition for maintaining fiscal prudence over the years. De-linking the minimum pension from the minimum wage – a proposal that is supported by influential members of the government's coalition – and setting a minimum retirement age for private-sector employees, preferably the same as that already in place for public-sector workers, and changing the eligibility conditions for retirement for women, are likely to be part of the agenda of reform over the next 10 years.

Reducing the tax burden

As the government successfully contains the increase in current outlays and improves the quality of public expenditure in the years to come, it will have to cut back to some extent Brazil's tax burden to promote job creation and growth. The tax burden reached over 35% of GDP in 2004 compared with 25% of GDP in 1993. Also, Brazil's tax burden is considerably higher than that of other

CHALLENGES TO FISCAL ADJUSTMENT IN LATIN AMERICA – ISBN 9264022074 © OECD 2006

Figure 4.5. **Government spending on pensions and the minimum wage, 1994-2004**

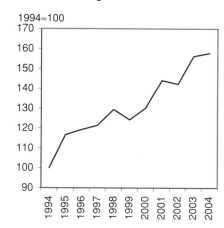

A. Pension benefits (INSS)

B. Minimum wage[1]

1.   Deflated by the IPCA.
Source: Statistical Yearbook of Social Security and IBGE.

Table 4.6. **New urban pensions, 2003**

Age at retirement	In % of new urban pensions
Less than 45 years	3.7
Less than 50 years	23.9
Less than 55 years	60.5

Source: Statistical Yearbook of Social Security.

emerging countries, which are typically lower than 20% of GDP, such as Chile (17%) and Mexico (18%). Brazil's tax burden is comparable to that of developed countries, such as Germany (36%), United Kingdom (37%) and Canada (35%), but without the same level of public services and economic infrastructure. Also, Brazil's tax system is immensely complex and inefficient. Reducing the tax burden is a pre-requisite for improving the quality of fiscal adjustment, which has so far relied more on tax increases than containing expenditure. This will by no means be an easy task, which is related to the more fundamental policy question about the appropriateness of the size of the public sector and the quality of its services and economic infrastructure.

Comments

Juan Carlos Lerda,
University of Chile

Introduction

The excellent contribution by Fabio Giambiagi and Marcio Ronci reviews the main structural and institutional fiscal reforms that took place in Brazil during 1995-2004 and discusses the main challenges to be faced by future administrations to ensure fiscal sustainability. My comments will focus on the latter topic.

The challenges for Brazil

I would like to emphasise the importance of price stability for ensuring fiscal sustainability in countries with a long history of chronic inflation. In the case of Brazil, numerous attempts to tame inflation prior to, and following the approval of, the 1988 Constitution had failed until the *Real* Plan of 1994 put in place the necessary conditions for macroeconomic reform. For the first time in years it was possible for the economic agents to base their inter-temporal decisions on hard-budget constraints and informed cost/benefit analysis. The reduction of inflation therefore put an end to the short-termism that prevailed during 1975-94 and discouraged private investment. Although it is often taken for granted, Brazil's history of low inflation is only ten years' old. The experience of the twentieth century suggests that even hyperinflation can reoccur in some countries; hence, low inflation cannot be taken for granted.

The authors underscore the importance of price stability by referring to the *Real* Plan in the first line of their Introduction. Nevertheless, it is important to emphasise that almost none of the fiscal reforms mentioned in the chapter could have been successful without the benefit of price stability. Therefore, the first and most important challenge for entrenching fiscal sustainability in Brazil is to

CHALLENGES TO FISCAL ADJUSTMENT IN LATIN AMERICA – ISBN 9264022074 © OECD 2006

maintain price stability over time, a task that usually requires a good deal more than fiscal discipline at all levels of government.

An equally important consideration is the possibility of creating "fiscal space" to accommodate additional pressure for increasing social expenditure (current and capital) at different layers of government in the years to come. These pressures are likely to arise given the need to reduce Brazil's poverty and indigence indicators, as well as improving its income distribution. An additional reason relates to political pressure, which might arise when the expectations created by the government when presenting its social programmes as a "silver bullet" for solving deeply rooted social problems are not fulfilled. Given the fact that Brazil's tax burden is already high and likely to rise further, an increase in primary expenditures may pose an obstacle to the attainment of the annual primary budget surplus targets.

Options for entrenching fiscal discipline

Fabio Giambiagi and Marcio Ronci offer two options for entrenching fiscal discipline in Brazil. The first involves the introduction of a "Fiscal Solvency Law", complementary to the Fiscal Responsibility Law, which would set a floor for the primary budget surplus or a ceiling for the headline budget deficit. This idea is akin to the Stability and Growth Pact (SGP), which complements the Maastricht Treaty. It is therefore useful to assess whether the SGP has in fact contributed to entrenching fiscal austerity among the member-countries of the European Economic and Monetary Union (EMU).

The SGP calls for balanced budgets over the medium term and sets a ceiling of 3% of GDP for the annual budget deficit. However, the SGP has been poorly enforced and lacks political support, as evidenced by Romano Prodi's, President of the European Commission, statement that "le pact de stabilité est stupide" in an interview with the French newspaper Le Monde in October 2002. In fact, the behaviour of most countries seems compatible with that view and, when faced with domestic pressures, several governments did not shy away from breaching the fiscal rule (the outstanding case being Germany, that in 2005 will complete 4 years with deficits above the ceiling), failing to report accurate fiscal data to Eurostat, as in the cases of Portugal in 2002 (when a new administration acknowledged that the budget deficit reported in 2001 was not 2.2 but 4.1% of GDP) and Greece in 2004 (when the budget deficit during 2000-03 was revised upward by approximately 2% of GDP), and basing budget projections on overoptimistic estimates of the pace of economic growth (therefore implicitly assuming a faster economic recovery than warranted by the data), and making frequent use of "one-off" measures and other types of fiscal gimmickry to delay the political costs of corrective action.[11]

These examples illustrate the reaction by policymakers to what they perceive as a negative externality associated with a formal fiscal straitjacket. When this reaction becomes widespread among countries that are expected to exert peer pressure on each other, the task of entrenching fiscal discipline through a "top-down" approach based on domestic legislation and/or international agreements, even under favourable economic circumstances, usually faces very tough, perhaps insurmountable, political resistance. Some recent decisions by the Economic and Financial Affairs Council (Ecofin) not to impose sanctions on countries that have repeatedly exceeded the annual deficit ceiling of 3% of GDP illustrates this point. The initiative to soften, rather than effectively enforce, the SGP provisions can do little to boost credibility in the fiscal rule. Summing up, as the European experience suggests, it certainly takes more than passing a law and/or signing a (federal or supranational) pact to effectively entrench fiscal discipline among fiscal authorities in different layers of government. The Brazilian Fiscal Responsibility Law of 2000 owes at least in part its undeniable success to the wise decision by the lawmakers to avoid setting a floor (cap) for the annual budget surplus (deficit).

The second option mentioned by the authors consists of maintaining the current policy aimed at generating primary budget surpluses in the neighbourhood of 4-5% of GDP for as long as necessary to bring the public debt-to-GDP ratio to a level that is acceptable by the markets and consistent with the amount of "debt intolerance" faced by Brazil. The authors consider this option politically more palatable, although it is vulnerable to discretion by future administrations, especially against a background where, as mentioned above, pressure for increasing social expenditure is likely to rise. Once again, failure to resist such pressures may put the maintenance of fiscal prudence at risk. I would argue that it is politically difficult for any incoming administration to continue to generate sizeable primary budget surpluses, despite the adverse effect of such a policy on economic growth and job generation in the formal sector. Some may argue that these policies are not only socially and politically untenable, but also inadequate from an inter-temporal point of view.

Notes

1. For a detailed account of the two Cardoso administrations see Gianbiagi and Ronci (2005).

2. Efforts to strengthen state finances started in 1993 when Mr. Cardoso was finance minister at end of the Collor administration. Two important initiatives were put in place. On 17 March 1993, a constitutional amendment was passed allowing the states to pledge their own revenue and the revenue

CHALLENGES TO FISCAL ADJUSTMENT IN LATIN AMERICA – ISBN 9264022074 © OECD 2006

transfers from the central government as collateral in their debt restructuring agreements with the federal government. This amendment was instrumental for debt restructuring and allowed subsequent challenges by the states in the Supreme Court to be defeated. On 5 November 1993, Law 8 727 was passed allowing the central government to refinance the debt that the states had outstanding with the federal banks, provided that the states pledged at least 11% of their net revenue for debt service and allowed the use of transfers from the central government as collateral. The first debt agreements under the provisions of this law were signed in 1994. On 30 November 1995, the National Monetary Council approved Resolution No. 162/95, which for the first time conditioned state debt rescheduling on compliance with fiscal targets. These three measures paved the way for the 1997 law that allowed the refinancing of the remaining state debts still in the market and the bonded debt that the states had with their own banks and in the market, with an increase in the minimum payment from 11 to 13-15% of net revenue (Giambiagi and Ronci, 2005).

3   Previously, pensions were calculated on the basis of length of service, which considerably reduced the retirement age and increased the costs of social security borne by the government.

4.   See Gianbiagi and Ronci (2005) for more information.

5.   For a detailed account of the first two years of Lula's administration see Giambiagi (2004).

6.   Inflation is measured by the IPCA index, calculated by the Brazilian Institute of Geography and Statistics (IBGE).

7.   Several empirical studies suggest that the debt threshold is somewhere between 30-40% of GDP, depending on the country's policy track record, with lower levels tolerated for countries that have a high debt ratio or have defaulted on their public debt obligations. Reinhart *et al.* (2003) find that more than one-half of the debt default episodes in their sample occurs at debt ratios below 60% of GDP, which would suggest that this is the maximum tolerable debt level for most countries.

8.   The change in the debt-to-GDP ratio over a period is equal to the accumulated new borrowing, less the accumulated amortisation payments and the change in nominal GDP, as shown in the formula:

$$\Delta(D_t/Y_t) = \Delta D_t/Y_t - (D_t/Y_t) * (\Delta Y_t/Y_t) \text{ or } \Delta(D_t/Y_t) = B_t/Y_t - A_t/Y_t - (D_t/Y_{t-1}) * (\Delta Y_t/Y_t),$$

where D is the stock of debt, ΔD is the change in D between $t\text{-}1$ and t, Y is nominal GDP, ΔY is the change in GDP between $t\text{-}1$ and t, B is borrowing between $t\text{-}1$ and t, and A refers to debt amortisation between $t\text{-}1$ and t. Therefore, if nominal GDP grows by a modest 6% a year, the initial debt-to-GDP ratio is 0.7 and the government maintains the PSBR at 3% of GDP ($B_t/Y_t - A_t/Y_t$), the public debt-to-GDP ratio would decline from 70% to 50% in 10 years.

9.   The high public debt-to-GDP ratio is offset by a relatively low corporate debt-to-equity ratio. This is fortunate, as the government could carry out voluntary, market-driven liability management to achieve a credible restructuring of the public debt with little impact on the financial market. See Vieira de Faria (2003, p. 54).

10.   One of the reasons why the social security system's balance sheet deteriorated is the women's right to retire five years earlier than men, which applies to both old-age (60 years versus 65 years) and length-of-service pensions (30 years versus 35 years). Also, women have longer life expectancy than men. Both factors tend to increase social security costs and reduce social security contributions (Giambiagi et al., 2004).

11.   See Koen and van den Noord (2005).

CHALLENGES TO FISCAL ADJUSTMENT IN LATIN AMERICA – ISBN 9264022074 © OECD 2006

Bibliography

Giambiagi, F. (2004), "Rompendo com a Ruptura: O Governo Lula", in F. Giambiagi, A. Villela, L. Barros de Castro and J. Hermann (eds.), *Economia Brasileira Contemporânea: 1945/2004*, Editora Campus, Rio de Janeiro.

Giambiagi, F., J.L. de Oliveira Mendonça, K.I. Beltrão and V.L. Ardeo (2004), "Diagnóstico da Previdência Social no Brasil: O Que Foi Feito e o que Falta Reformar?" *Texto para Discussão*, No. 1050, Instituto de Pesquisa Econômica Aplicada (IPEA), Rio de Janeiro.

Giambiagi, F. and M. Ronci (2005), "Brazilian Fiscal Institutions: Cardoso's Reforms, 1995-2002," *CEPAL Review*, No. 85, April, pp. 59-77.

Koen, V. and P. van den Noord (2005), "Fiscal Gimmickry in Europe: One-Off Measures and Creative Accounting", February, *OECD Economics Department Working Paper*, No. 417, Paris.

Reinhart, C., K. Rogoff and M. Savastano (2003), "Debt Intolerance", *NBER Working Paper*, No. W9908, NBER, Cambridge, MA.

Vieira de Faria, L. (2003), "Financial Markets, External Shocks and Policy Responses: The Case of Brazil 2001", *Brazilian Journal of Political Economy*, Vol. 23, No. 4.

Chapter 5

Structural change in Chile: From fiscal deficits to surpluses

José Pablo Arellano*

Fundación Chile

This chapter discusses the driving forces behind Chile's strong fiscal performance. It is argued that fiscal rectitude owes much to the progressive concentration of policymaking powers on the executive branch of government, including over sub-national finances. The ban on revenue earmarking is highlighted as a means of rendering fiscal management more flexible. Structural reform since the return to democracy in 1990 was facilitated by a high degree of political cohesiveness. The use of fiscal policy as a demand management instrument is due to the introduction of mechanisms to deal with the impact on the budget of fluctuations in copper prices and the business cycle, an achievement that is underpinned by Chile's low level of public indebtedness.

*   This paper is part of the CIEPLAN research programme. I am grateful to Mario Marcel, Carlos Salineros and Rene Cortazar for comments but remain the sole responsible for any errors and omissions.

Introduction

One of the strengths of the Chilean economy is its fiscal performance. Several indicators are worth pointing out: the public debt-to-GDP ratio fell from 45% in 1990 to 13% in 2004.[1] The budget has been in surplus almost without interruption, averaging 1% of GDP between 1987 and 2004.[2] Exceptionally, a deficit was recorded in 1999-2003 when growth slowed down and the price of copper fell sharply. Measured in cyclically-adjusted terms, a budget surplus was nevertheless posted in the period. At the same time, country risk has been reduced and is now among the lowest among the emerging-market economies. Chile is rated among the top performers in international competitiveness rankings on account of its fiscal policy. This has nevertheless not always been the case. The average budget deficit was 1.9% of GDP between 1950-86, except for just five years of surplus and public indebtedness was on the rise.[3]

The fiscal consolidation effort of the last 18 years has been a key instrument for reducing inflation and ensuring high economic growth. Fiscal policy has ceased to be a cause of macroeconomic imbalance; it has permitted the adoption of a counter-cyclical policy stance, which has brought about greater stability of growth and employment in the face of external shocks. Thanks to the reduction in public indebtedness and the improvement in fiscal performance, the country was able to cope better with the negative effects of the Asian crisis in the late 1990s and, in part, to mitigate these effects. At the same time, fiscal policy has made it possible to set medium-term objectives for social development and public investment which is difficult in situations of fiscal weakness. Not only was social spending not reduced at the time but it has also continued to rise uninterruptedly.[4]

The main focus of this chapter is to identify the factors behind this structural change. The objective is not to provide a detailed historical account of Chile's economic performance but, rather, to underscore the key engines of reform. The analysis also contributes to the study of fiscal outcomes from a comparative cross-country perspective,[5] and is based in part on my personal experience when in charge of the national budget from the return of democracy in 1990 to the end of 1996, and as an active observer thereafter from other parts of government that also involve the use of public resources.

The constitutional and legal framework for fiscal policymaking

A key determinant of fiscal performance is to the way in which policymaking powers are distributed among the various stakeholders and the rules governing the formulation, approval and implementation of the budget. For many decades, it was common in Chile for the Presidents to blame

CHALLENGES TO FISCAL ADJUSTMENT IN LATIN AMERICA – ISBN 9264022074 © OECD 2006

pervasive deficits and fiscal imbalances on the fact that they had no authority over expenditure policy and the public finances in a way they considered appropriate from the point of view of macroeconomic management.

Starting in 1925, legal and constitutional reforms progressively reinforced the authority of the executive branch of government in fiscal policy. The 1925 Constitution adopted a presidential regime, which was strengthened in 1943 during the Juan Antonio Ríos' administration, with the approval of a constitutional reform giving the executive branch stronger prerogatives in public spending. In practice, however, this was not enough. All the subsequent Presidents, Carlos Ibáñez del Campo, Jorge Alessandri and Eduardo Frei Montalva, elected with the support of different political parties, proposed constitutional reforms which would strengthen presidential authority in expenditure matters. Jorge Alessandri, in the constitutional reform law of July 1964, stated that:

"The steadily growing importance of economic and social problems and the consequent pressure exerted by Congress in these matters highlight the need to introduce changes to the 1925 Constitution with a view of protecting the country's fiscal stability. To this end, only the President of the Republic should be able to take the initiative to propose legislation is related to the remuneration of public-sector workers. This was the purpose of the reform of the Constitution in 1943 and during the presidency of Juan Antonio Ríos. Unquestionably, its spirit was also to tackle budgetary problems and that was the view taken by Congress before I took office".

"What has happened since the 1943 amendment has suggested that much more radical changes are needed to remedy the problem. Those inappropriate practices that were previously introduced by Congress under the Budget Law nowadays make their presence felt in all the laws which the executive branch submits for its consideration, especially those of a social, budgetary, financial and tax nature and others, apart from the fact that Congressmen very often propose legislation on these subjects which give rise to even worse outcomes. Each law is the subject of hundreds of provisions which undermine its purpose and other legislation in force, and involve all kinds of matters totally alien to the law itself".

"The consequences of all these initiatives fall on the President of the Republic, who is responsible for the financial and economic administration of the nation. If the President has sole responsibility for its management, the logical consequence is that Congressmen should not have any right of initiative whatsoever in this matter and that such a right should belong exclusively to the Head of State. In other words, for all these problems, the same principle which inspired the 1925 Constitution concerning the national budget law should prevail. Only thus can anarchy, injustice and privilege in wage policy be avoided in the public or the private sectors, and a budgetary system free of favouritism, a tax system and an investment policy can be established and maintained in accordance with a harmonious development plan for the national economy. It is therefore sought to avoid the bad practice whereby Congress allocates through the budget law funds for specific works, which has been one of the major reasons why it has been impossible to implement public investment programmes as economically and rapidly as possible…".[6]

Jorge Alessandri did not succeed in securing congressional approval for his constitutional reform, which led Eduardo Frei Montalva to propose soon after taking office in November 1964 that "there is an urgent need to reserve to the executive branch the initiative in all laws which involve expenditure or which have an impact on the economy". In particular:

"This measure is rooted in the economic reality of our times. There is no doubt that the enormous complexity of the modern economy and the need to plan investment and set targets and priorities demands not only short-term planning but also long-term development, which requires a unified approach to investment and expenditure. To this end, it is essential to ensure that pre-established targets, objectives and priorities are not undermined by contradictory initiatives. Once the economic and social policy objectives have been approved, it is up to the government to implement them, which means that it must be given the exclusive initiative in all legislation which involves expenditure or other measures which may interfere with the implementation of plans or programmes. This is what the law I am presenting to you seeks to achieve when it extends in article 45 the matters of law where the initiative is reserved exclusively to the President of the Republic".

Almost six years had passed before this constitutional reform was approved in 1970 at the end of Eduardo Frei Montalva's term in office. On the occasion of the promulgation of the reform, President Frei Montalva stated that "the authority of the executive branch must be reaffirmed with respect to the planning and control of the economy and, to that end, it is necessary to extend the scope of legislation which is of the exclusive initiative of the President of the Republic, to all matters which impact on fiscal expenditure and the system of remuneration and pensions in the private sector. The idea exists already in the current Constitution, under the reform sponsored by President Ríos. It is imperative because the efficient management of the economy, which involves all sectors, requires that this responsibility be based in the executive branch which, by its structure and the technical assistance available to it, is in a position to act with the consistency and continuity that the National Congress

CHALLENGES TO FISCAL ADJUSTMENT IN LATIN AMERICA – ISBN 9264022074 © OECD 2006

cannot provide and which are essential in all countries, but especially those like ours which are developing".

The text approved by Congress was the following (Law No. 17 284 of 23 January 1970): "It shall be the exclusive prerogative of the President of the Republic to propose amendments to the Budget Law to alter the country's political or administrative structure; to abolish, reduce or waive taxes or contributions of any kind, interest or penalties, defer or consolidate their payment and grant total or partial tax exemptions; to create new public services or paid employment; to modify the remuneration and other pecuniary benefits of staff in the public administration, both central and local; to fix minimum wages or salaries for workers in the private sector, increase their remuneration on a mandatory basis or alter the rules by which they are determined; to create or modify pension and social security entitlements; and to grant or increase, *ex gratia*, retirement, old-age or survivors' pensions or *ex gratia* pensions. These provisions shall not apply to Congress and services under its authority".

The military government which took power in the midst of a serious fiscal crisis introduced a series of changes to centralise policymaking powers over public revenue and expenditure in the Treasury. These measures were summarised in a new law on the financial administration of the State (Decree Law 1263) which came into force in 1975.[7] This law incorporated all revenue and expenditure in the national budget and abolished practically all earmarking of tax revenue. In 1980, the new Constitution reinforced the provisions of the previous constitutional reforms which had been approved in 1943 and 1970: budgetary and financial management prerogatives were concentrated in the President of the Republic.

To sum up, successive legal and constitutional reforms strengthened the authority of the executive branch of government in fiscal matters leading to the current legal framework enshrined in the 1980 Constitution and in the 1975 Financial Administration Law (as subsequently amended), which underscored and extended presidential authority over fiscal policymaking. According to the constitutional provisions currently in place, it is the exclusive prerogative of the President of the Republic to propose legislation on tax and expenditure matters, including those of a budgetary character.

With regard to the budget-making process, the main provisions of current legislation are as follows. The national budget presented by the executive branch to Congress must be approved within 60 days prior to 30 November of each year. The estimation of revenue is the exclusive responsibility of the executive branch. Congress can only reduce the expenditure envelope proposed in the draft budget law and does not have the prerogative to reallocate resources in the draft budget law without the executive branch's agreement. If Congress does not approve the budget law within the constitutional timeframe, the law comes into force as presented by the executive branch. At the same time, the legislation on financial management calls on the Treasury and the Budget Office to take the lead in the drafting, discussion and implementation of the budget. Borrowing must be authorised by the Treasury for all public entities, including corporations, and is banned for the municipalities, unless authorised by law.

In the Chilean tradition, the executive branch has political responsibility for the economic management and administration of the State. This institutional framework has underscored a fairly strong tradition of fiscal discipline where different ministries are subject to the authority that, in practice, Presidents delegate to the Treasury to conduct fiscal policy. This system, which concentrates policymaking powers, makes it possible for the government to set objectives for fiscal policy and not to leave fiscal performance to the mercy of generally independent, and not necessarily mutually consistent, decisions taken by different stakeholders.

Fiscal policy is the most political of economic policies. It requires the capacity to exercise self-discipline in the face of multiple demands and needs, numerous beneficiaries and interest groups, and scarce resources. Only with very good institutions and rules can fiscal policy become an effective instrument of macroeconomic management. In my view, the constitutional and legal reforms that were implemented by successive administrations and emerged with full clarity in the current rules are the main factors explaining the strong fiscal performance of the last 18 years. Comparison with other countries leads to similar conclusions as can be drawn from our history: legislation that encourages the centralisation of, and a strong hierarchical system for, decision-making delivers better fiscal outcomes.[8]

Budget institutions and fiscal performance

Unity and comprehensiveness of the budget

All revenue and expenditure, and all entities except the public enterprises and the municipalities, are included in the budget approved by Congress. Before the 1975 Financial Administration Law, some revenue, borrowing and expenditure items were often treated off-budget. As a result of this practice, there were different *fora* for negotiation and decision-making concerning the total amount of revenue and expenditure, which made it difficult for the fiscal authorities to achieve the desired budgetary outcomes.[9] The counterpart of comprehensiveness is greater flexibility in execution, allowing the reallocation

CHALLENGES TO FISCAL ADJUSTMENT IN LATIN AMERICA – ISBN 9264022074 © OECD 2006

of budgetary funds in line with financial management needs. Revenue and expenditure programmes are approved in the budget law at a fairly aggregate level; that is, there is only one line for payroll, another one for outlays on goods and services, and a few lines for transfers when different programmes are identified.

Strengthening the tax system

A pre-requisite for sound fiscal policy is a tax system that is capable of collecting the resources needed to finance the budgeted expenditure envelope. This requires laws that clearly define the tax bases and allow for efficient tax administration. In this respect, the Chilean tax system has been evolving over time. Collection performance was affected adversely by inflation, which eroded the real value of the tax take, a phenomenon that was mitigated in part by the introduction of indexation in the 1960s. In the current tax regime, in place since 1975, taxes are fully indexed to a unit of account, which is regularly updated based on inflation measured by the CPI for the previous month. This means that the tax take is fully protected against inflation.

In addition, as a result of indexation, tax legislation takes on a permanent character and does not have to be revised for every budget. In fact, budget laws do not include any tax provisions, in addition to the estimates of the tax take that will be generated based on unchanged legislation. This makes it possible to formulate tax policy from a medium- and long-term perspective and not with respect to the financing needs of any particular budget.

There has been a sustained improvement in tax administration over the last 20 years, significantly reducing evasion. The capacity of the Internal Revenue Service was enhanced by giving it greater powers of control and to close loopholes in the tax code, which could facilitate tax evasion and/or avoidance.[10] The quality of tax administration in terms of the probity and dedication of its staff and the increasing use of the new information technologies have made it one of the most modern in the world. With regard to the effects of the tax system on the allocation of resources, although not the subject of this chapter, disincentives and distortions are minimised because of the neutrality of the tax code.

During the last ten years there has been a major change in the structure of tax revenue to accommodate the successive reductions in import tariff to an average of 2% as a result of bilateral free-trade agreements. This has reduced the share of revenue from taxes on foreign trade from 10% to 1.5% of tax collections. Another important development from the macroeconomic point of view has been the prohibition by law of the earmarking of tax revenue for specific expenditure items.[11] Revenue earmarking creates rigidities and prevents the allocation of resources according to changing priorities and macroeconomic objectives. Of course, taxes are created to meet specific needs and, as such, the introduction of new taxes needs to be justified in the legislative process on the basis of the specific use for the funds they raise. However, this is very different from earmarking the revenue of a tax whose base and amount collected will change over time. The earmarking of taxes may also stem from pressures exerted by interest groups; the absence of earmarking therefore prevents transitory legislative victories from translating themselves into permanent measures which are difficult to reverse. The current constitutional provision which prevents revenue earmarking is thus most useful.

Capacity to control borrowing

The counterpart to deficits is borrowing; it is therefore important for fiscal policymakers to have centralised control over the financial operations of public entities. Under the current legal framework, entities that are part of the central government require authorisation by the Treasury to borrow. Relationships with multilateral lending organisations (*e.g.* World Bank, Inter-American Development Bank) is centralised at the Budget Office. Public enterprises, whose budget is not approved by law but by Treasury order, require authorisation from the Treasury to contract loans. The municipalities, which have budgetary autonomy, may not borrow unless authorised to do so by law. The executive branch of government has not proposed any law to authorise municipal borrowing in the last fifteen years.

The 1992 Regional Government Law banned regional government borrowing. The explicit objective of this reform was to encourage the decentralisation of investment without the risk of losing control over public borrowing and the fiscal policy objectives set by the central government. For this reason, while granting increased fiscal powers to the regional governments, including the prerogative to formulate their own budget, special care was taken to ensure that the Treasury's ability to control the overall level of expenditure was not jeopardised. The new role of regional governments involved greater autonomy to allocate resources to different investment projects, but within a centrally determined framework. As a result, the proportion of public investment that is allocated at the regional level increased from 18% in 1992 to almost 50% now.

The legislation which limits borrowing is complemented by strict control on the part of the banking supervision authorities. As new mechanisms for private investment have developed based on concessions, the government has provided guarantees to reduce risk and facilitate private investment. These

120

contingent liabilities cannot be provided without the authorisation of the Treasury. In support of transparency and higher accounting standards, a register of contingent liabilities of the public sector has recently been created setting out the government's commitments under public-private partnership contracts.[12]

Political consensus on the importance of fiscal discipline: The lesson from macro-economic crises

In a democratic environment, there is support for the rule of law to the extent that it is perceived as serving the common interest; instead of that of individual groups. Otherwise, laws end up facing resistance and being amended. There has been general consensus on this matter over the last 15 years, despite some reaction on the part of lawmakers against their lack of power in the budget process. Since the return to democracy, the institutional framework for discussing and approving the budget has been enhanced and the quality and quantity of information available to this end has improved steadily.[13] The legal framework has been maintained and improved through the budget law and amendments to the Financial Administration Law.[14] The rules setting the powers and authority of stakeholders have focused on the macroeconomic objectives of the budget and fiscal policy.[15] This is evidenced by the functioning of the Copper Stabilisation Fund and the fiscal policy rule, discussed below.

Behind this political consensus is the recognition of the importance of fiscal discipline and the high price paid by the country in the past in periods of fiscal imbalance and macroeconomic crisis. At the same time, fiscal discipline has paid off, generating a "fiscal dividend". The reduction of government borrowing, for example, has allowed a firm response to external crises, and lower interest payments have freed up resources to finance social spending.

With the return to democracy in 1990, the main factor behind cohesiveness within the centre-left coalition government was the need to avoid fiscal relaxation and the resurgence of macroeconomic imbalances. The political crisis of 1973 and the economic crisis of 1982-84 were associated with costly macroeconomic disarray, which was very much present in the memory of all stakeholders. In those days, those who might have disagreed with the conduct of fiscal policy or the main elements of the institutional framework for policymaking described above yielded to the consensus to avoid instability. Subsequently, policies gradually proved to be effective, generating dividends that contributed to entrenching the consensus, particularly due to its ability to sustain social spending in the face of external difficulties, to reduce inflation and country risk, and to give the policy framework greater predictability.

Fiscal sustainability: The Copper Stabilisation Fund and the structural budget surplus rule

The Copper Stabilisation Fund was created in 1987 and the structural budget surplus rule in 2001. Both mechanisms sought to anchor fiscal policymaking in a longer-term framework. It is worth examining their impact on fiscal policy.

The Copper Stabilisation Fund

Copper price cycles have traditionally had a strong impact on government revenue in Chile. The share of copper has varied between 5 and 17% of tax collection.[16] To counter the effect of variations in the price of copper, a stabilisation fund was created and has been in operation since 1987.[17] The basic idea is to save resources when the price of copper exceeds its long-term level so as to use these savings when copper prices fall below the long-term trend. The operational rules of the Copper Stabilisation Fund and the trend in assets during the last 15 years are presented in Annex 5.1).

The Copper Stabilisation Fund prevents expenditure from increasing beyond the level deemed sustainable over the medium term and provides financing to ensure its continuity when prices fall. Before this mechanism came into effect, public expenditure usually rose in boom years in line with the rise in revenue, but it was difficult to reduce it when prices came down, a phenomenon described by Rogelio Arellano and Fausto Hernández in Chapter 6 for the case of oil in Mexico. Currently, the resources accumulated in the Fund are used to retire external debt. To the extent that debt is reduced during booms, spending on debt service can subsequently be reduced in bad times. As a result, markets also have greater confidence in policies, without the fear that the debt dynamics may become unsustainable.[18] Chile is therefore among the few countries in the world that can implement fiscal policy in a counter-cyclical manner, thereby alleviating the magnitude of the natural resource price cycle. In times of crisis, the room for manoeuvre is very limited and thus the government is often unable to implement counter-cyclical policies.

The structural budget surplus rule

In 2001, the mechanism for stabilising fluctuations in the price of copper was complemented by another mechanism to deal with fluctuations in revenue arising from deviations of GDP growth from its long-term trend. A methodology was set up for estimating revenue based on trend GDP growth, so that expenditure can be calculated on the basis of the government's capacity to collect taxes over the medium term, rather than on economic conditions each

CHALLENGES TO FISCAL ADJUSTMENT IN LATIN AMERICA – ISBN 9264022074 © OECD 2006

year. Fiscal policy objectives are therefore set consistent with the budget's structural balance. As a result, not only can fiscal policy be implemented in line with long-term revenue trends, but the introduction of a fiscal policy rule targeting a structural budget surplus of 1% of GDP has allowed for counter-cyclicality.[19]

Where it is possible to have a counter-cyclical fiscal stance, the degree to which it is appropriate to do so will be open to debate. It is certain that in the midst of a crisis there will be a natural tendency to press for the maximum use of counter-cyclical measures. The structural budget surplus rule addresses this challenge and enhances credibility by setting a clear *ex ante* limit on counter-cyclical measures. In recent years, the rule has allowed for fairly significant counter-cyclicality. In 2001 and 2002, the budget balance based on the fiscal rule was between -0.5 and -1.2% of GDP. In both years, the Copper Fund allowed the financing of expenditure equivalent to 1% of GDP.

These stabilisation mechanisms serve an important political purpose. They set priorities and play an educational role by targeting an explicit level for the budget balance. They also imply a political commitment by the authorities to a fiscal objective and hence reduce the need for negotiating the level of the desired budget balance each year. Moreover, they strengthen fiscal discipline by rendering budget outcomes that deviate from the level set by the fiscal rule costlier. These mechanisms contribute to the sharing of political responsibilities and make it easier for policymakers to bear the political burden of not being able to meet social demands in a low-revenue environment and to limit the benefit of spending revenue windfalls in boom years. By setting a formal budget target, the rule reduces discretion, since it can always be argued that the special circumstances of each economic cycle would justify a more expansionary policy. The automatic nature of the rule can overcome difficulties in reaching agreements in situations of change in parliamentary majority and where there is greater political competition. For the same reason, these mechanisms facilitate the implementation of fiscal policy, making it swifter, compared with what would happen if the fiscal measures were fully discretionary.

Such a rule, once it has gained credibility, can send a signal of sustainability to financial markets, generating benefits in terms of access to, and costs of, financing. A discretionary policy, on the other hand, presupposes greater ability by the economic authority to persuade markets that the current policy stance is the most appropriate from the macroeconomic point of view and thus justifiable in terms of the particular characteristics of each business cycle. Because credibility is important, indeed indispensable for sound economic policymaking, this rule enhances the credibility of fiscal policy and macroeconomic policy in general, by making it more effective and reducing adjustment costs. These stabilisation mechanisms have contributed to creating a common ground on what is acceptable and desirable in fiscal policy. These mechanisms not only give medium-term sustainability to fiscal policy, with all the benefits that have been described, but they also extend the planning horizon. It is possible to design and implement medium-term initiatives without the extreme uncertainty of their budgetary sustainability, as was so common in past decades and in countries which have not achieved fiscal sustainability.

It is interesting to note that neither the Copper Stabilisation Fund nor the structural budget surplus rule are set in law. These mechanisms are good policies which the executive branch of government has introduced, whose legitimacy has been justified in practice, and whose specific application has been improved over time. An improvement to gain credibility and strengthen these rules was the initiative put in place in 2002 that the key parameters for estimating the long-term price of copper and trend GDP growth used to set the structural surplus, should be determined by a panel of independent experts. The panel adds credibility and dispels any doubts concerning the discretionality to which this type of mechanism may be exposed.

Market discipline and monetary policy autonomy

A complementary factor which contributes to fiscal discipline is provided by the financial markets and monetary policy. The autonomy of the Central Bank of Chile since 1989 means that the monetary authorities are formally independent of the fiscal authorities and can therefore evaluate the macroeconomic effect of fiscal stance. If the monetary authorities consider it more expansionary than desirable from the point of view of price stability, they can raise interest rates, generating a cost for fiscal policy. A similar role is played by the financial markets when they evaluate the sustainability of fiscal policy, which affects country risk and, thus, the cost of finance.

The autonomy of monetary authorities and the role of financial markets are new elements reinforcing fiscal discipline but, based on Chile's experience, they have not been the decisive factors. They have consolidated the achievements on the fiscal area: the autonomy of monetary policy and the role of financial markets cannot lead to a structural change from bad to good fiscal policy, but once the change has taken place, they reinforce and consolidate it.

Conclusion

There has been a growing recognition of the role of institution in economic analysis. The improvement in macroeconomic performance in Chile, and in particular the dramatic change in fiscal policy, is a clear example of the

CHALLENGES TO FISCAL ADJUSTMENT IN LATIN AMERICA – ISBN 9264022074 © OECD 2006

importance of institutional change, resulting in a sustained move from chronic deficits to structural surpluses. This move has allowed the country to reap a fiscal dividend, leading to greater stability and higher growth. It has also been reflected in better quality of the services financed by the State. Parallel to the good macroeconomic performance, it has been possible to achieve a more redistributive fiscal policy. Many challenges remain, but there is no doubt that fiscal discipline makes it possible to concentrate efforts and energies to improve the quality of public services.

Comments

Joaquim Oliveira Martins,

OECD Economics Department

The development challenge and policy complementarities

Pablo Arellano's chapter describes a remarkable achievement in terms of fiscal discipline and consolidation and discusses how these institutions have contributed to the stability of the Chilean economy. Nonetheless, the overall good performance and the functioning market institutions should not overshadow the fact that Chile still faces the challenge of finding a sustained and equitable development path. Notably, social demands will be pressing in many areas and these pressures may be exacerbated by a relatively unequal society.

Much in the same way that convergence in income levels requires sustained and coordinated reforms supporting the growth potential of the economy, a sustainable structural fiscal surplus must be the result of appropriate macro-structural complementarities, in particular between fiscal and social policies. Indeed, liberal policy packages require strong internal coherence. In my comments, I would like to highlight three key interactions between fiscal and social policy areas.

The pension reform may not prevent future social contingent liabilities

A first example of policy complementarities is the pension system. While Chile has implemented a major reform of the pension system, a dual labour market may create contingent liabilities hindering the structural fiscal position. As discussed in OECD (2003b), the fully-funded pension system in Chile may not be immune to the problem of ageing because of the significant informality and low density of contributions (in part due to the large share of agricultural employment and seasonal activities).

CHALLENGES TO FISCAL ADJUSTMENT IN LATIN AMERICA – ISBN 9264022074 © OECD 2006

Without major changes in labour market conditions enhancing business incentives to hire formal labour, improved co-ordination between health care and pension policies, better functioning of the pension market, as well as a more diversified economic structure, old-age assistance benefits may end up creating again a burden on fiscal accounts. If these policy synergies do not materialise, the Chilean government may be obliged to redesign the basic pillar in terms of its size and financing sources.

Moreover, to reduce the spending pressures associated with old-age poverty, Chile needs to further develop the segments of its financial markets, such as annuity markets, that adequately ensure longevity risks (as an aside, this issue also applies to most OECD countries).

Health care may also create structural expenditure pressures

Another area requiring careful reform design is the health sector. Major reforms are under way, such as the AUGE Plan, which will increase the participation of the public sector in the provision of health services. This is desirable to tackle inequality and inefficiencies in the present system, but cost containment in this area will be essential.

Health expenditures have a natural tendency to increase with income per capita. While the magnitude of this income elasticity is still subject to much debate, the evidence available to date would suggest at least a unitary value. This implies that no reduction in the relative share of health expenditures to GDP can be expected from fast economic growth. In addition, technological improvements often reduce the unit costs of treatments but stimulate coverage and increase overall demand, so that technical progress is another important source of cost pressures.[1] Population ageing will also be an important driver of expenditures, as the country is facing a rapid demographic transition.

Insofar as universal health coverage may create perverse incentives for low participation and informality in the lower income groups, the interactions of health reforms with the labour market and the pension system should be carefully analysed.

With an increase of the elderly segment of the population, the demand for long-term care is likely to rise rapidly. Currently, most of old-age long-term care is provided informally, within family networks. Nevertheless, if Chile aims at increasing significantly the participation of women and young people in the

---

1.   For a discussion of the main drivers of health expenditures in OECD countries see Jacobzone (2000) and Jacobzone *et al.* (2003).

labour market, the availability of such informal services is likely to decline in the future. This is another policy interaction that requires attention.

Spending in education: from coverage to quality

Progress has been made in increasing access, coverage and reducing repetition rates. These reforms in the education system were supported, among others, by the use of education vouchers; the full-day school (*jornada completa*); the increase in the age of compulsory education from 8 to 12 years; and targeted programmes for low performing students and schools, and improving quality.

Despite all these efforts, the quality is still low, as shown by the results of the OECD/PISA+ exercise (OECD, 2003b, Chapter V). As the development of the Chilean economy requires a large and continued investment in human capital formation, the quality of public spending in this area is essential to ensure a sustainable policy path.

To sum-up, while Chile's macroeconomic policies are praiseworthy, especially in a region marked by recent turbulence and instability, there are structural factors to be addressed in order to reinforce a lasting commitment towards fiscal stability. In particular, despite a relatively low tax-to-GDP ratio, the size of the state is a controversial issue, so more focus on the quality of social spending may be required. Policy complementarities are often viewed as a political constraint, but could on the contrary become a source of benefits by reinforcing the returns from the Chilean liberal model.

Notes

1.   The net debt fell even more markedly from 30% of GDP in 1990 to -0.3% of GDP in 1998, reaching 4% of GDP in 2004. The public debt statistics are available at www.dipres.cl.

2.   The central government budget includes all public entities except corporations and the municipalities. The budget balance is measured on a cash basis. More information on public finance statistics is available at www.dipres.cl.

3.	This refers to the Treasury deficit, see Central Bank of Chile (2002), French-Davis (1973) and Wagner, Jofré and Lüders (2000).

4.	For more information on social policy and its relationship with fiscal policy, see Arellano (2005).

5.	See Persson and Tabellini (1999) for a survey of the literature.

6.	In the reform it is proposed "… that the President should have the exclusive prerogative to impose taxes of any class or nature, abolish, reduce, set exemptions or amend any form of existing taxes, indicate as appropriate their distribution between the provinces or municipalities and determine their form, proportionality or progression, contract loans, or engage in any other class of transactions which might compromise the creditworthiness or financial responsibility of the State, semi-fiscal entities, autonomous provincial or municipal enterprises and cancel, reduce or modify bonds, interest or other financial charges of any kind, established in favour of the Treasury or any other of the aforementioned organisations or entities; to create new public services or paid employment, whether fiscal, semi-fiscal, autonomous, in provincial or municipal enterprises, to grant *ex gratia* pensions, and in general, any law which implies expenditure by the Treasury. The President will also have exclusive initiative concerning laws on social security or which have an impact thereon, both in the public and the private sectors, and those which set or increase wages, salaries, gratuities or emoluments, remuneration or loans of any kind to employees in service or pensioners in the private sector. The National Congress may only accept, reduce or reject services, employment, emoluments, loans, benefits, expenditure, increases and other initiatives proposed to which the two previous paragraphs refer".

7.	This law replaced Decree Law DFL 47 of 1959.

8.	"Comparisons between countries suggest that … centralisation of budgetary authority in the prime minister or the minister of finance … restrictions in the possibility of amending expenditure … seem to produce greater fiscal discipline" (Persson and Tabellini, 1999, p. 62). A recent study for OECD countries (OECD, 2003a), concludes that the character of fiscal policy is influenced by the institutional framework which regulates it and that it tends to be pro-cyclical in situations where decision-making is fragmented. It is noteworthy that, despite the rules governing the drafting and approval of budgets, only in the last 15 years has its importance been recognised in studies on the subject. Up to the late 1980s, comparative studies of budgetary practices did not exist even in the member-countries of the European Union.

9.   Until 1975, the budget of the autonomous and decentralised agencies were approved by decree generally during the budget period, making overall control of public spending difficult.

10.   For a review of initiatives to combat evasion during 1990-2005 see http://www.sii.cl/aprenda_sobre_impuestos/estudios/adminis_tributaria.htm

11.   The only exception is the copper revenue that is earmarked for the armed forces. There is a growing consensus towards phasing out this exception.

12.   For an estimate of these liabilities at the end of 2003 see http://www.dipres.cl/presupuesto/documentos/Informe_Finanzas_Publicas_2004.html.

13.   See IMF (2003) for more information on fiscal transparency.

14.   Law 19 908 of October 2003, for example, extends the borrowing control provisions to swaps. Law 19 896 of September 2003 establishes regular reporting requirements.

15.   See the positive evaluation of an OECD mission requested by the authorities to examine budgetary practices (OECD, 2004).

16.   On the importance of copper see Meller (2002).

17.   In 1981, under Decree Law No. 3 653, a copper reference price mechanism was established to allocate revenue above the reference level to debt payments.

18.   OECD (2004) argues that, for several of the OECD countries, fiscal policy became more pro-cyclical in the 1980s and 1990s due to the fact that the accumulation of public debt prevented the application of expansionary in cyclical downturns.

19.   For a description of the structural budget surplus rule see Marcel et al. (2001), Marcel and Tokman (2002) and Ministry of Finance (2001).

Bibliography

Alesina, A., R. Hausmann, R. Hommes and E. Stein (1999), "Budget Institutions and Fiscal Performance in Latin America", *Journal of Development Economics*, Vol. 59, pp. 253-73.

Alesina, A. and R. Perotti (1999), "Budget Deficits and Budget Institutions", in J. Poterba and J. von Hagen (eds.), *Fiscal Institutions and Fiscal Performance*, University of Chicago Press, Chicago, Il.

Alesina, A. and R. Perotti, (1995), "The Political Economy of Budget Deficits", *IMF Staff Papers*, Vol 42, No. 1, pp. 1-31.

Arellano, J.P. (2005), "Políticas Sociales para el Crecimiento con Equidad Chile 1990-2002", *El Trimestre Económico*, Vol. 72, No. 2, pp. 409-49.

Budget Office, *Public Finance Statistics*, Ministry of Finance, Santiago, www.dipres.cl.

Central Bank of Chile (2002), *Economic and Social Indicators, 1960-2000*, Central Bank of Chile, Santiago.

French-Davis, R. (1973), *Políticas Económicas en Chile: 1952-70*, Ediciones Nueva Universidad, Santiago.

International Monetary Fund (2003), "Chile – Report on the Observance of Standards and Codes (ROSC), Fiscal Transparency Module", IMF, Washington, D.C.

Jacobzone, S. (2003), "Ageing and the Challenges of New Technologies: Can OECD Social and Health Care Systems Provide for the Future?", *The Geneva Papers on Risk and Insurance*, Vol. 28, pp. 254-74.

Jacobzone, S., E. Cambois and J.M. Robine (2000), "Is the Health of Older Persons in the OECD Countries Improving Fast Enough to Compensate for Population Ageing?", *OECD Economic Studies*, No. 30, Paris.

Marcel, M. and M. Tokman (2002), "Building a Consensus for Fiscal Reform: The Chilean Case", *OECD Journal on Budgeting*, Vol. 2, No. 3, pp. 35-55.

Marcel, M., M. Tokman, R. Valdés and P. Benavides (2001), "Balance Estructural del Gobierno Central Metodología y Estimaciones para Chile: 1987-2000", *Estudios de Finanzas Públicas*, September, Ministry of Finance, Santiago.

Meller, P. (ed.) (2002), *Dilemas y Debates en Torno al Cobre*, Dolmen Ediciones, Santiago.

Ministry of Finance (2001), "Exposición sobre el Estado de la Hacienda Pública", Ministry of Finance, Santiago.

OECD (2003a), *Economic Outlook*, No. 74, Chapter IV, OECD, Paris.

OECD (2003b), *Economic Survey of Chile*, OECD, Paris.

OECD (2004), "Budgeting in Chile", paper presented at 25th Annual Meeting of Senior Budget Officials, OECD, 9-10 June, Madrid.

OECD Economics Department (2004), *Economics Newsletter*, Issue 2, June, OECD, Paris.

Persson, T. and G. Tabellini (1999), "Political Economics and Public Finance", *NBER Working Paper*, No. 7097, NBER, Cambridge, MA.

Vial, J. (2001), "Institucionalidad y Desempeño Fiscal: Una Mirada a la Experiencia Chilena en los 90", *Serie Estudios Socio/Económicos*, No. 5, CIEPLAN, Santiago.

Wagner, G, J. Jofré and R. Lüders (2000), "Economía Chilena 1810-1995. Cuentas Fiscales", *Working Paper*, No. 188, Institute of Economics, Pontifical Catholic University of Chile, Santiago.

Annex 5.1

The Copper Stabilisation Fund

The Copper Stabilisation Fund was established in 1987 following a crisis in the first half of the decade. It was an old idea which had never been implemented formally. The justification for a stabilisation fund is that the price of copper fluctuates enormously and fiscal revenue from the profits of CODELCO, the state enterprise which produces and exports copper, represents some 5% of current government revenue and the bulk of its foreign currency earnings.

The system operates as follows. A reference price is fixed in advance for each year taking into account the estimated medium-term trends or the most stable price. In the 1990s, the reference price was fixed by the Ministry of Finance. From 2001, and to make it independent from the fiscal authorities, an expert committee was set up to recommend the reference price to be used in the budget (Table 5.A1.1). If the actual price in a given year exceeds the reference price by up to 4 cents of US dollar, the corresponding revenue windfall is used freely. For the next 6 cents, 50% of the surplus revenue must be saved. If the gap between the actual and reference prices is above US$ 0.1, these resources are saved into the Copper Fund. If the actual price is below the reference price, the rules apply symmetrically: for the first 4 cents, the authorities are not allowed to access the fund, for the following 6 cents, up to 50% of the revenue shortfall may be transferred from the Fund, and above 10%, the Treasury may fully compensate the revenue shortfall through transfers from the Fund. The calculations are made quarterly, taking into account actual CODELCO sales and export prices. The funds are held in an account with the central bank, which is responsible for the financial management of these resources.

There is enough flexibility in the use of funds. There was concern at the return to democracy about fiscal irresponsibility, leading the democratically-elected government to disburse all the resources at the end of 1989 to repay public debt. In 1990, as a result of the geopolitical tension in the Gulf and the sharp rise in oil prices, part of the Copper Fund assets was used to create an Oil Stabilisation Fund, with the obligation to return the resources to the Copper Fund when international oil prices fell. To a large extent this was done. In subsequent years, public debt was reduced. Not only did new borrowing decline considerably but foreign debt was also repaid early. Throughout the period, no resort was made to domestic borrowing. Given the conditions of those loans, early repayment was a good financial investment. Public debt fell from 47.2% of GDP in 1990 to 14.2% of GDP in 2000. The external public debt fell from US$ 12.25 billion 1989 to US$ 5.3 billion at the end of 2000.

It is worth emphasising that the copper price stabilisation mechanism is not set in law. Naturally, it is included annually in the Budget Law and Congress is provided with a report of the financial performance of the Fund. In general, it has been given a low profile and the Budget Law only notes the resources that may be expended. Since 2002 the reference prices have been fixed by a committee of experts whose reports can be seen at www.dipres.cl.

Table 5.A1.1. **Copper prices and Stabilisation Fund operations, 1987-2004**

| | Copper price (in US$ per pound) | | Copper Fund balance (in US$ million) | | | |
	Reference	Actual	Revenue	Disburse-ments	Net revenue	Balance
1987	61.5	81.1	26.3	0.0	26.3	26.3
1988	71.0	117.9	496.0	439.5	56.5	82.8
1989	75.0	129.1	1203.0	1260.1	-57.1	25.7
1990	79.0	120.9	785.1	256.2	528.9	554.6
1991	82.0	106.1	289.7	200.0	89.7	644.3
1992	93.0	103.6	134.6	0.0	134.6	778.9
1993	96.0	86.7	9.8	39.0	-29.2	749.8
1994	96.0	104.9	46.5	101.4	-54.9	701.5
1995	96.0	133.2	664.3	0.0	664.3	1365.7
1996	96.0	103.9	324.4	7.3	317.1	1682.8
1997	96.0	103.2	117.6	0.0	117.6	1800.5
1998	96.0	75.0	3.8	273.5	-269.7	1530.7
1999	92.0	71.4	63.4	516.0	-452.6	1078.2
2000	92.0	82.3	0.0	404.8	-404.8	673.4
2001	92.0	71.6	250.0	302.3	-52.3	621.1
2002	90.0	70.6	138.9	483.0	-344.1	277.0
2003	88.0	80.7	0.0	202.5	-202.5	74.6
2004	88.0	130.0	..	..	..	207.8

Source: Budget Office and Central Bank of Chile.

CHALLENGES TO FISCAL ADJUSTMENT IN LATIN AMERICA – ISBN 9264022074 © OECD 2006

Chapter 6

Challenges of Mexican fiscal policy

Rogelio Arellano Cadena   and   Fausto Hernández Trillo*

Bank of Mexico   CIDE

This chapter reviews the Mexican experience with fiscal adjustment. Different scenarios are presented for Mexico's debt dynamics, arguing that the country has been relatively successful at containing expenditure pressures, while facing important challenges for the future. These include the need to ensure fiscal sustainability over the longer term, given the remaining unrecorded contingent liabilities associated with the public enterprises and the pension system, and to boost revenue performance, against a backdrop of continued reliance on oil revenue. The chapter also discusses the microeconomic aspects of fiscal adjustment, focusing on the need for improving the cost-effectiveness of government spending on infrastructure and social programmes.

*   We thank the participants of the OECD Seminar in Fiscal Adjustment in Latin America, held in Paris on 10 November 2004, for helpful comments, and especially to Luiz de Mello, Bénédicte Larre and Alfredo Cuevas. The views expressed here do not necessarily represent those of the institutions to which the authors are affiliated.

Introduction

Mexico posted large budget deficits during the 1970s and early 1980s, reaching 16% of GDP in 1982, the highest in recent history. When the Debt crisis erupted in 1982, macroeconomic adjustment was achieved through the implementation of an orthodox programme at first, followed by some heterodoxy, as an economic pact was reached to control prices in all sectors. These adjustment programmes included strong fiscal consolidation. Since then, Mexico's fiscal policy has been conducted in a prudent manner, including after the Tequila crisis of 1994, when the value added tax (VAT) rate was raised from 10 to 15%.[1] Fiscal discipline has been accompanied by responsible monetary policymaking since 1993, when the central bank was granted formal independence. The Mexican authorities have been relatively effective at containing the growth of expenditure in support of fiscal consolidation, but, as we show in this chapter, reliance on oil revenue may pose some pressure to aggregate demand, which in turn affects inflation.

There are important challenges in the fiscal area, including the need to ensure fiscal sustainability over the medium-to-longer term, to raise tax collection, including by reducing reliance on oil revenue (the "Fiscal Dutch Disease"), and to pursue structural and microeconomic reform. This chapter will address these three challenges.

Fiscal performance and debt sustainability

Fiscal versus monetary dominance

The issue of fiscal versus monetary dominance has been recognised in the literature, although it remains open to theoretical debate. Traditional monetary theory argues that inflation is a purely monetary phenomenon and, hence, fiscal policy does not affect the dynamics of inflation. Assuming that markets are complete and that Ricardian equivalence holds, fiscal deficits do not affect aggregate demand. Thus, under monetary dominance, an appropriate monetary stance that credibly signals an inflation path would be enough to keep inflation under control. In other words, fiscal policy has to ensure that the public sector is solvent for any monetary policy path (Liviatan, 2003). Woodford (2001) nevertheless casts doubt over this proposition.

Under fiscal dominance, the fiscal stance is supported by the monetary authority so that the effectiveness and credibility of monetary policy are jeopardised by fiscal imbalances (*e.g.* unsustainable expansionary policy or debt dynamics).[2] In this setting, the price level is determined by fiscal policy, and the

CHALLENGES TO FISCAL ADJUSTMENT IN LATIN AMERICA – ISBN 9264022074 © OECD 2006

monetary authority is forced to generate the *seignorage* and inflation-tax revenue needed to maintain fiscal solvency. Fiscal policy can therefore affect the price level even when an autonomous central bank sets monetary policy independently of the fiscal stance (Woodford, 2001). Given that non-Ricardian fiscal regimes are possible, explicit or implicit fiscal rules are needed to maintain macroeconomic stability. Therefore, central banks must abide by monetary rules that are consistent with the fiscal policy regime in place. This clearly implies that the choice of policy regime is important to achieve price stability.

Fiscal dominance and the risk it poses for price stability can be mitigated by fiscal rules with the primary objective of making macroeconomic policies credible. A good example of such rules is the European Union's Stability and Growth Pact, which explicitly acknowledges "…the objective of sound government finances as a means of strengthening the conditions for price stability and for strong sustainable growth conducive to employment creation".[3] Fiscal rules have also been put in place in emerging market economies. For example, Chile has a structural budget surplus rule of 1% of GDP, while Brazil introduced comprehensive fiscal responsibility legislation in 2000, calling for annual primary surplus targets (currently at 4¼ per cent of GDP for the consolidated public sector) and setting ceilings for sub-national public indebtedness.[4]

Debt sustainability

Mexico has followed a prudent fiscal policy over the last two decades, especially since the 1990s. The primary budget balance has been in surplus for the whole period (Table 6.1). As a result, the public debt-to-GDP ratio has fallen, helped by the maintenance of low interest rates abroad since the 2000 recession. Government spending on debt service has fallen from nearly 5% of GDP in 1995 to about 1.5% of GDP in 2003. Also, the average maturity of the public debt has increased substantially, with a substitution of domestic debt for external debt, which reduces exchange rate risk (Figure 6.1).

At about 47% of GDP in 2003, the public debt is sustainable. Mexico has liabilities associated with the restructuring of the banking system and the toll roads, which are included in the debt statistics. Also, the government has relied on public-private partnerships to finance investment on energy infrastructure (PIDIREGAS) since 1997. These partnerships may create contingent liabilities for the budget and, therefore, expenditure pressures.[5] While these outlays are recorded in the public sector borrowing requirements (PSBR), they will only be

Table 6.1. **Public sector budget outturn, 1995-2003**
In per cent of GDP

	1995	2000	2001	2002	2003
Budgetary revenue	22.8	21.6	21.9	22.1	23.2
Federal government	15.2	15.8	16.2	15.8	16.4
Tax revenue	9.3	10.6	11.3	11.6	11.1
Non-tax revenue	6.0	5.2	4.9	4.2	5.3
Public enterprises and entities	7.6	5.8	5.7	6.4	6.8
Budgetary expenditure	23.0	22.7	22.6	23.3	23.9
Programmable expenditure	15.4	15.7	15.9	16.9	17.6
Non-programmable expenditure	7.6	7.1	6.7	6.4	6.3
Primary budgetary expenditure	18.4	19.1	19.3	20.5	21.1
Primary economic balance	4.4	2.6	2.5	1.7	2.1

Source: Bank of Mexico.

Figure 6.1. **Average maturity of public debt, 1995-2003**
In days

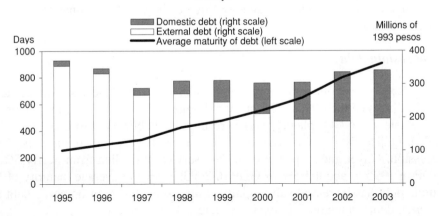

Source: Bank of Mexico.

recorded above-the-line when payments are actually made (Table 6.2). In addition, other unrecognised contingent liabilities include those associated with the public enterprises – PEMEX (the national oil company), CFE (the national electricity company), IMSS (the Social Security Institute) and ISSSTE (the Public Sector Social Security Institute) – the sub-national governments and the pension system for federal civil servants. It is hard to estimate exactly the level of these liabilities (Table 6.3), but they are thought to be high in proportion of

Table 6.2. **Public sector borrowing requirements (PSBR)**
In per cent of GDP

	2002	2003
PSBR	-2.66	-0.61
Conventional balance	-1.23	-0.15
PIDIREGAS	-0.80	-0.26
IPAB	-0.46	-0.07
Budgetary adequacies	-0.25	-0.03
Highways Fund (FARAC)	-0.43	-0.01
Debtors Programme	0.08	0.00
Development Banking and other Funds	0.42	-0.09
Non-recurrent revenues	0.71	0.17
Memorandum items:		
PSBR excluding non-recurrent revenues	-3.37	-0.78

Source: *Secretaria de Hacienda y Crédito Público*.

Table 6.3. **Contingent liabilities, 2003**
In per cent of GDP

	Conservative estimate	Alternative estimate
Total	85	156
ISSSTE	50	60
Sub-national governments' pensions systems	12	31
Public enterprises	20	60
Public universities	3	5

Source: CIDE, World Bank, IMF and author's calculations.

GDP. The stock of unrecognised contingent liabilities could in principle decrease through pension reform.

Assessing fiscal sustainability

In short, one of the main issues of concern regarding Mexican fiscal policy and its adjustment is the sustainability of public finances. This problem has been addressed many studies and for several countries, including Hamilton and Flavin (1986), Wilcox (1989), Buiter (1990), Ahmed and Rogers (1995), Uctum and Wickens (1996) and Talvi and Végh (2000). These authors propose different methodologies for testing for fiscal sustainability. It is not the purpose of this chapter to examine all of them; instead, the methodology proposed by Talvi and Végh (2000) will be used for the Mexican case (Annex 6.1).[6]

Before presenting the simulations, it should be noted that the IMF has calculated a "corrected primary balance" for Mexico which takes into account many flows of funds associated with contingent liabilities, such as *PIDIREGAS*, as well as those related to the toll roads. These figures are not published by the federal government. The IMF calculations suggest that the corrected primary balance was 1.8% of GDP in 2000, 0.8% of GDP in 2001 and 0.3% of GDP in 2003.

Different scenarios are presented in Table 6.4 for Mexico's debt dynamics. In the conservative scenario, the level of debt is set at 47% of GDP, the observed level in 2003 excluding contingent liabilities. An alternative debt level is set at 170% of GDP, taking into account the average level of all contingent liabilities discussed above, in addition to the observed level of indebtedness (47%). These simulations are sensitive to the parameters used in the analysis. The worst possible scenario arises when the economy grows at 2% per year in real terms, the interest rate is set at 6% in real terms and the debt level is 170% of GDP. In this case, the "corrected" primary budget surplus would have to be nearly 7% of GDP, relative to the average outturn of 0.8% of GDP over the last three years. On the other hand, the least conservative scenario is when contingent liabilities are not taken into account and real GDP grows at 5% per

Table 6.4. **Public debt simulation**
In per cent

Debt-to-GDP ratio	Real growth rate	Real interest rate	Regional primary balance-to-GDP ratio
47	2	5	1.4
47	3	5	1.0
47	4	6	1.0
47	5	6	0.5
170	2	6	6.9
170	3	6	5.3
170	4	5	1.8
170	5	6	1.8

Source: Author's calculations.

CHALLENGES TO FISCAL ADJUSTMENT IN LATIN AMERICA – ISBN 9264022074 © OECD 2006

year, resulting in a required primary budget surplus of 0.5% of GDP. These simulations suggest that the current level of indebtedness is sustainable. However, debt would become unsustainable, should contingent liabilities arise in the future. It is true that pension liabilities do not build up overnight, but a higher required primary balance would be needed to ensure fiscal sustainability over the longer term, which would imply a reallocation of budgetary funds away from poverty alleviation and public infrastructure programmes.

Alternatively, the methodology can be used to calculate the maximum debt-to-GDP ratio for different primary surplus levels. As in CIDE-ITAM (2003), the simulations suggest that the current primary surplus of 0.3% of GDP, combined with a rate of growth of GDP of 4% per year, would be associated with a debt-to-GDP ratio of 14.4%. A higher primary surplus, at 0.8% of GDP (the average outturn during the Fox administration, 2001-03), coupled with a GDP growth rate of 4%, would result in a debt level of nearly 75% of GDP. Again, should contingent liabilities be taken into consideration, the public debt overhang would become unsustainable. It is important to note that the debt statistics refer to the federal government only, thereby excluding the explicit and contingent liabilities of the sub-national layers of government.[7]

Reliance on oil revenue and its effect on aggregate demand

Mexico relies heavily on oil revenue (Figure 6.2). At about 11% of GDP (excluding oil revenue) and around 18% of GDP (including social security contributions) Mexico's revenue-to-GDP ratio is among the lowest in the OECD area. The main channel through which oil affects government expenditure is the setting of its *ex ante* reference price for estimating oil revenue and, subsequently, the expenditure envelope. If this reference price turns out to be higher *ex post* than originally set, then the higher-than-expected excess oil revenue, coupled with any non-oil revenue windfall, make up what is referred to as "the total net excess revenue".

The total net excess revenue is allocated according to a predetermined formula, which has been adjusted over the years. Typically, most of the oil revenue is used to finance public expenditure, while only a small fraction of it is deposited in the Oil Stabilisation Fund, which received less than 9% of total net excess revenues in 2003, and its balance was only US$ 558 million (less than 0.1% of GDP). The fact that oil revenue windfalls have been used to finance predominantly current, rather than capital, expenditure (Figure 6.3) is at odds with the public finance principle that non-recurrent revenue should be invested in activities that yield a future return, social or economic, so that their benefits are distributed among different generations by smoothing consumption over time.

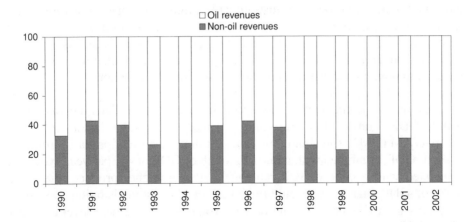

Figure 6.2. **Composition of revenue, 1990-2002**
In per cent

Source: Ministry of Finance.

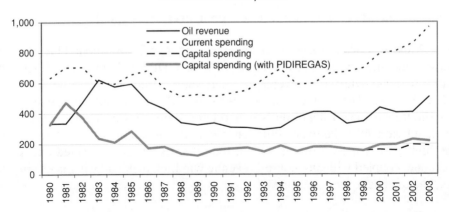

Figure 6.3. **Oil revenue and government spending, 1980-2003**
In billions of 1993 *pesos*

Source: Ministry of Finance.

In order to formally estimate the relationship between oil revenue and government spending, co-integration tests were carried out using monthly data for the period January 1984 to June 2004. The empirical findings (not reported) suggest that oil revenue co-integrates with current outlays, but not with capital expenditure.[8] These results suggest that, not only is a cut in expenditure likely to occur in the event of a negative oil price shock, but also a considerable proportion of oil revenue is used to finance current expenditure, which may

CHALLENGES TO FISCAL ADJUSTMENT IN LATIN AMERICA – ISBN 9264022074 © OECD 2006

affect public finances adversely over the medium term. Based on these results, there has been an increase in government expenditure in previous years associated with the surge in oil revenue. Therefore, the transitory nature of the favourable oil shock has exerted pressure on the fiscal stance.

To shed further light on the impact that reliance on oil revenue has on aggregate demand, the expanded operational balance (EOB) (Blejer and Cheasty, 1991) was calculated.[9] The EOB includes expenditure that is not recorded in the budget, such as *PIDIREGAS*, and, more importantly, excludes revenue items, such as oil duties paid by foreigners, because they do not affect domestic demand.[10] Calculation of the EOB (Figure 6.4) shows a stronger upward trend than that of the primary budget balance since 1996. It is also interesting to note that, in 2003, the headline budget deficit declined while the primary budget surplus increased, which can be interpreted as a negative effect of the fiscal stance on the economy. However, the EOB had quite a different trend, rising from 4.1% of GDP to 6.3% of GDP.

Therefore, contrary to what alternative fiscal measures might suggest, increasing oil-related revenue, of which a high proportion comes from abroad, has put upward pressure on expenditure, thereby boosting domestic demand and inflation. This result is in line with the co-integration analysis presented above. A second important challenge facing Mexico is hence to reduce fiscal dominance, by relying less on oil revenue and more on non-oil receipts, and redirecting oil revenue to finance long-term capital expenditure, spreading the benefits of "windfall" gains to future generations. This is known in the Mexican

Figure 6.4. **Indicators of fiscal policy stance, 1990-2004**
In per cent of GDP (a negative number indicates a budget surplus)

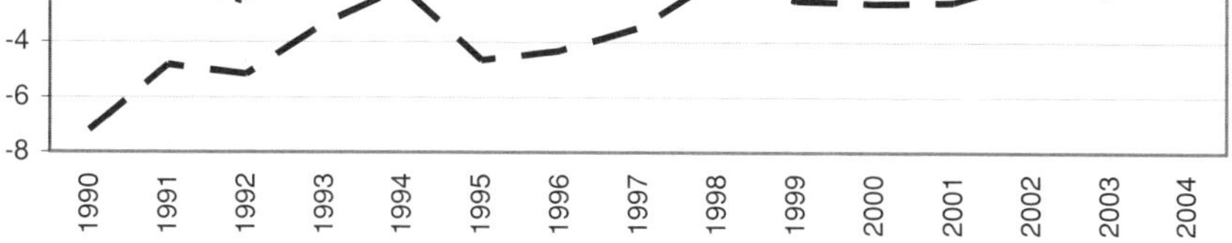

Source: Ministry of Finance and Bank of Mexico.

case as the "Fiscal Dutch Disease", where excess oil revenue has discouraged the authorities from collecting taxes from non-oil sources and implementing fiscal reform (Hernández and Zamudio, 2004).

The microeconomic effects of Mexican fiscal policy

This section assesses Mexico's revenue and expenditure patterns from the point of view of income distribution and resource allocation.

Revenue and expenditure

As discussed above, revenue is low as a share of GDP and biased in favour of oil sources, which makes it highly volatile and affects expenditure policy and management. The composition of tax revenue is also tilted towards indirect taxes (Table 6.5). Revenue from taxes on income and value added accounts for more than 80% of total tax collection. Tax rates are competitive internationally, especially with respect to the NAFTA countries, but collection is low. Revenue from the corporate and personal income taxes amount to less than 5% of GDP, compared to an average of 13.5% of GDP in the OECD area. Revenue from the value-added tax accounts for less than 4% of GDP, against almost 7% of GDP in the OECD area on average. VAT productivity is therefore estimated at only 0.22, as opposed to 0.40 for the OECD countries on average.[11]

There are various reasons for Mexico's low revenue mobilisation capacity. Hernández and Zamudio (2004) conclude that 38% of potential VAT revenue (2% of GDP) is forgone because of tax avoidance or evasion. Tax avoidance is due to special treatments and loopholes in legislation, while evasion can be

Table 6.5. **Non-oil federal tax revenue, 2002**
In per cent of GDP

	2002
Total	10.8
Tax revenue	10.3
Income tax	4.9
VAT	3.8
Non-oil excises	0.5
Imports	0.6
Other taxes	0.5
Non-tax revenue	0.5

Source: *Secretaria de Hacienda y Crédito Público.*

attributed to poor tax administration and corruption. The option of greater reliance on taxes on consumption should be considered, as these taxes tend to have higher revenue-raising capacity.

The composition of federal expenditure (excluding the public enterprises) has changed over time (Figure 6.5). Transfers increased dramatically over the past decade, mostly towards the sub-national governments, the pension system and the public enterprises. The first important increase was in 1992-93, when federal teachers were transferred to the state governments, resulting in a reduction in the federal wage bill and an increase in transfers from the federal to the state governments to pay for teacher salaries. Transfers rose again in 1997-98, when part of the health care system and social expenditure were decentralised and *Ramo 33* was created to aggregate all the earmarked allocations to the sub-national governments. This increase in transfers was accompanied by a reduction in capital expenditure and spending on central government wages, goods and services, and general services, among other items. Debt service declined dramatically as a consequence of debt restructuring during the Salinas administration (1988-94). Outlays on goods and services, which are the lowest spending item, also declined, but this level of expenditure is probably not sustainable, given their importance in service delivery for complementing investment and personnel expenditure. This pattern is not significantly different for the public enterprises (Figure 6.6). Capital expenditure is low and is being displaced over time by spending on pensions.

Figure 6.5. **Composition of federal spending: Economic classification, 1990-2004**
In per cent

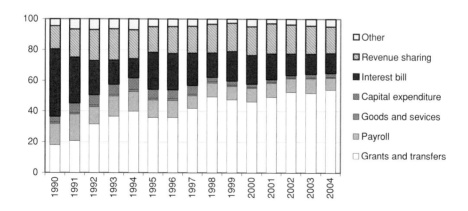

Source: Secretaría de Hacienda y Crédito Público.

Figure 6.6. Composition of expenditure: Public enterprises, 1990-2004
In per cent

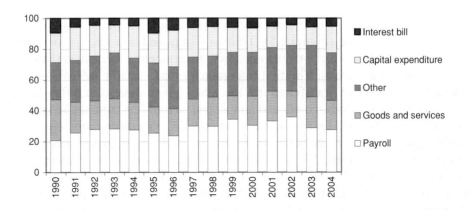

Source: *Secretaría de Hacienda y Crédito Público.*

Public infrastructure

Total infrastructure investment dropped from an average of over 2% of GDP in the previous two decades to around 1% of GDP in the late 1990s. Of the major Latin American countries, Mexico now has one of the lowest levels of total infrastructure investment as a share of GDP, against 5-6% of GDP in Chile in the late 1990s, 6-7% of GDP in Colombia and around 2% of GDP in Brazil (Easterly and Servén, 2003). Improving access to, and the quality of, infrastructure service, especially for the poor, will require not only higher levels of infrastructure investment, but also an effort to improve the efficiency of government spending on investment and subsequently on related operations and maintenance.

Inefficient infrastructure services have reduced Mexico's international competitiveness and hampered economic growth by driving up production costs. An estimated 18% of GDP is spent on logistics, including modal congestion (*e.g.* roads, bridges, seaports, and borders and other inland terminals) as well as the inefficiencies of "soft" transport infrastructure, such as customs clearance. In general, investment in basic infrastructure, such as electricity, transport and water, has fallen as a share of total government expenditure and in quality. In the case of transport, Mexico has a low road density (Table 6.6) and paved roads account for only one-third of total road infrastructure, against 99% in Spain and Thailand, for example. There is evidence that the electricity, water and oil sectors are also lagging behind in quality and quantity.[12]

CHALLENGES TO FISCAL ADJUSTMENT IN LATIN AMERICA – ISBN 9264022074 © OECD 2006

Tablo 6.6. **Tranoport infrastructure density and quality, 2002**

	Area (in millions of Km²) (A)	Roads (Km) (B)	Density (B)/(A)	Paved roads (in % of total)	Railway infrastructure index[1]	Port infrastructure index[1]
Spain	0.5	0.66	1.3	99.0	4.4	4.7
Greece	0.1	0.12	0.9	92.0	2.6	4.4
Portugal	0.1	0.07	0.8	86.0	3.9	..
USA	9.6	6.30	0.7	97.0	4.7	6.0
Malaysia	0.3	0.06	0.2	76.0	4.9	6.1
Brazil	8.5	1.80	0.2	6.0	2.2	3.3
China	9.6	1.70	0.2	91.0	3.7	3.7
Mexico	2.0	0.30	0.2	33.0	2.4	3.3
Chile	0.8	0.08	0.1	20.0	2.2	4.6
Thailand	0.5	0.06	0.1	99.0	3.7	4.5
Canada	10.0	0.90	0.1	35.0	5.1	5.9
Argentina	2.8	0.22	0.1	29.0	2.5	3.7

1. The higher the score on a 1-7 scale, the better the quality of infrastructure.
Source: World Economic Forum (*Global Competitiveness Report*, 2003-2004).

Another challenge to be addressed is the pricing policies for public infrastructure services. For example, tolls may be as high as US$ 0.30 per kilometre on some important roads, a level that is comparable to urban tunnels in the city of New York. Another example is the electricity subsidies, which are regressive and unevenly distributed across the regions, distorting relative prices and affecting comparative advantages (Dávila *et al.*, 2002). The incidence of the residential electricity subsidy, estimated by the World Bank using household expenditure survey data, became more even during 1996-2000 as a result not of a change in the tariff structure but of the extension of coverage in the lowest eight income deciles (Table 6.7). Between 2000-02, instead, the gain in progressivity was due to a large extent to the change in the tariff structure, which lowered subsidies significantly for the top income decile. Thus, while the increase in federal subsidy in the former period was distributed fairly equally (although biased against the poorest quintile), the reduction in subsidy in 2000-02 was absorbed by the better-off. As a result, while the 2002 tariff revision mitigated regressivity somewhat at the very top of the income distribution, the share of subsidies accruing to the non-poor (*i.e.* those above the poverty line) remains high, estimated at 64%.

Table 6.7. **Distribution of residential electricity subsidy by income decile, 1996–2002**

| | Average incidence (in per cent) | | Marginal incidence | | | |
| | | | Change in incidence (percentage points gained) | | Distribution of change in expenditure (participation in change) | |
	2000	2002	1996–2000	2000–02	1996–2000	2000–02
Lowest	2.7	3.4	0.5	0.7	6.0	-10.6
Second	4.3	4.8	-0.5	0.5	2.9	-5.5
Third	6.0	6.3	0.7	0.2	10.6	1.1
Fourth	6.9	7.2	-0.3	0.3	6.6	1.9
Fifth	8.9	9.8	0.6	0.9	12.4	-8.5
Sixth	9.6	11.4	0.7	1.8	14.0	-26.0
Seventh	11.5	12.1	0.8	0.6	15.5	-0.2
Eighth	13.5	13.1	0.4	-0.4	15.3	21.0
Ninth	16.4	16.4	-1.6	0.0	6.8	16.8
Highest	20.1	15.6	-1.3	-4.6	10.0	109.9
Memorandum items:						
Concentration coefficient	0.29	0.24	9.5	-17.7	..	..
Change in expenditure	..	..	..	..	22.5	-4.9

Source: INEGH and World Bank.

Poverty and income distribution

The cost-effectiveness of public social expenditure has to be assessed against a background of high poverty and income inequality. Poverty is pervasive: 20% of the Mexican population is extremely poor and 53% is poor. The poorest 10% of the population receive only 1.3% of national income, while the richest 10% receive 40% of national income. The Gini coefficient is 0.53 and has been persistently high. To reduce poverty and improve the distribution of income, the government relies on the tax system and transfers, monetary and in kind, as well as the provision of goods and services, such as education and health care. While monetary transfers redistribute current income, the provision of health care and education services creates equitable options for human capital accumulation, thus improving future earnings capacity. In mature welfare states, monetary transfers are the main policy instruments to redistribute income. In Mexico, these transfers represent a small proportion of redistributive

148   CHALLENGES TO FISCAL ADJUSTMENT IN LATIN AMERICA – ISBN 9264022074 © OECD 2006

expenditure, barely affecting the overall distribution of income. However, they are well targeted and, together with their conditionality for access to basic education and health care services, have an important redistributive impact on the incomes of the rural poor.

On the revenue side, the tax system is neutral/progressive (Dalsgaard, 2000). Based on the 2002 national income-expenditure survey, the income tax is estimated to be progressive (Hernandez and Zamudio, 2004). But the incidence of VAT is neutral, considering the number of zero-rated items and exemptions (Table 6.8). The experience of Mexico suggests that nearly 48% of the goods and services are zero-rated or exempted from VAT. This implicit subsidy is highly regressive: for each peso exempted from the poorest 20% of the population, nearly 5 *pesos* is exempted from the richest 20%. Hernandez and Zamudio (2004) estimated that this subsidy accounts for nearly 2% of GDP.

Combining the revenue and expenditure sides of the budget shows that the impact of fiscal policy on the distribution of income is only mildly progressive. Public expenditure on tertiary education is highly regressive, as expected. For example, in Chile, 36% of social expenditure reaches the poorest 20% of the population, whereas only 4% of expenditure reaches the wealthiest 20% of the population. The World Bank (2004) assessed the incidence of selected social programmes (Figure 6.7) suggesting that most are regressive. Perhaps the most striking observation is the broad range of coefficients, from 0.6 (ISSSTE

Table 6.8. **The incidence of value added taxation, 2002**

Income decile	Value added tax			All taxes
	Percentage of tax collection	Net payment (in % of household income)	Including exempted goods	Relative incidence (in %)
Lowest	1.5	11.4	5.2	0.9
Second	2.4	10.7	4.9	3.6
Third	3.3	10.4	5.1	5.7
Fourth	4.3	10.0	5.1	7.2
Fifth	5.6	9.3	5.3	8.1
Sixth	7.0	9.0	5.4	9.8
Seventh	9.0	8.6	5.5	10.5
Eight	10.9	8.8	5.3	11.2
Ninth	15.3	8.1	5.2	12.7
Highest	40.9	6.5	5.8	16.9

Source: INEGH.

Figure 6.7. **Selected social programmes: Concentration coefficients, 2000-02**

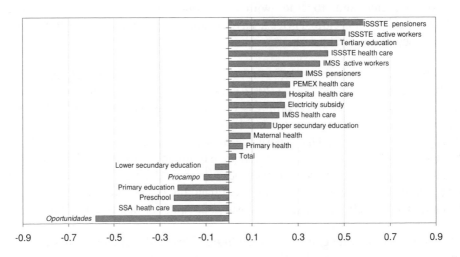

Source: Scott (2004).

pensions) to -0.6 (*Oportunidades*). Following *Oportunidades* at some distance, health services for the uninsured, basic education and *Procampo* are the only other programmes that are considered progressive. In general, these programmes are notably more progressive in urban than in rural areas, suggesting that most of their redistributive impact is due to the inter-sectoral allocation of funds, rather than the effectiveness of targeting the rural poor. Although *Oportunidades* remains the most progressive programme in rural areas, expenditure on rural primary schools are as effectively targeted as transfers under *Oportunidades*.

Conclusions

This chapter has shown that Mexico's public finances are managed adequately. There are, however, some areas for further improvement. The first is the accumulation of contingent liabilities, which are estimated to account for above 120% of GDP. The second is the excessive reliance on oil revenue, which may create challenges for the conduct of monetary policy and inflation targeting. Finally, the structure of social expenditure and the tax system are not conducive to income redistribution and poverty alleviation. The fiscal authorities should make an effort to raise tax revenue and to work on improving the efficiency of fiscal policy, including in the areas of expenditure, revenue and public debt management.

CHALLENGES TO FISCAL ADJUSTMENT IN LATIN AMERICA – ISBN 9264022074 © OECD 2006

Comments

Bénédicte Larre,

OECD Economics Department

Introduction

It is an interesting time to be discussing challenges for fiscal policy. As the figures below show, Mexico has achieved strong fiscal adjustment and has a relatively good record in maintaining fiscal discipline, notwithstanding unexpected cyclical developments and volatility in oil-related revenue. However, as argued by Rogelio Arellano and Fausto Hernández, looking beyond this seemingly good fiscal performance, there are important challenges ahead. Fiscal sustainability needs to be enhanced in the long run, tax collection needs to be strengthened, mitigating the budget's reliance on oil revenue, and a number of microeconomic challenges remain, notably on the spending side. My comments will address in some detail three related points: Mexico's fiscal policy performance, the dependency on oil-related revenue and the need for a medium-term approach to fiscal policy.

Mexico's fiscal performance from an OECD perspective

Over the past years, the Mexican authorities have managed to reduce the budget deficit, and fiscal outcomes have usually been closely in line with the targets; the more comprehensive public sector borrowing requirement (PSBR) was brought down to close to 3% of GDP in 2004 (about one-half of its 1999 level), and lower than the budget deficit of several major OECD countries (Figure 6.8). This record of fiscal discipline has helped the Mexican authorities to gain credibility, as demonstrated by the fact that international investors have decoupled Mexico from other Latin American countries. When the crises erupted in Russia, Brazil and Argentina (1998, 1999, 2001, respectively), Mexico suffered relatively less from contagion (Figure 6.9).

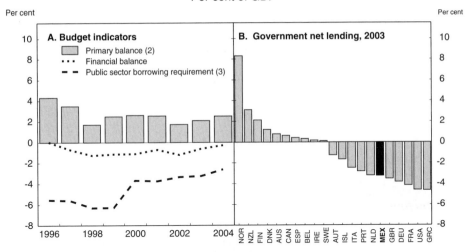

Figure 6.8. **Public sector budget indicators**[1]
Per cent of GDP

1. The public sector comprises federal government and public enterprises under budgetary control (such as PEMEX). Financial intermediation by development banks is not included.
2. The primary balance is the financial balance less net interest payments.
3. Public sector borrowing requirement (PSBR) includes net costs of "PIDIREGAS", inflation adjustment to indexed bonds, imputed interest on bank-restructuring and debtor-support programmes and financial requirements to development banks. Non-recurrent revenues (privatisation) are not included. Further adjustment to include the net non-recurrent capital costs of the financial sector support programmes would increase the PSBR

Source: Ministry of Finance; Banco de México; OECD, Economic Outlook database 76.

The net public sector debt was less than 25% of GDP in 2004, based on the traditional definition, and 45% of GDP, based on the broader definition that includes the net debt of the federal government, the non-financial public enterprises, the development banks and the official trust funds, as well as the liabilities related to banking-sector restructuring and PIDIREGAS, the Mexican-type public-private partnerships. Such a debt level is not high by OECD standards.

As noted by Rogelio Arellano and Fausto Hernández, these figures should be adjusted to include the liabilities related to public-sector pensions. But it should also be noted that Mexico is not alone regarding this problem; other OECD countries also have substantial liabilities from ageing populations. Although the OECD has not made precise estimates of additional debt for

CHALLENGES TO FISCAL ADJUSTMENT IN LATIN AMERICA – ISBN 9264022074 © OECD 2006

Figure 6.9. **Trend in risk premia (Discount Brady Bonds yield) in Mexico, Argentina and Brazil**

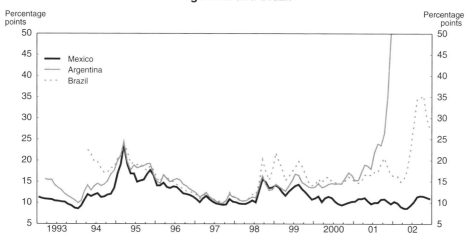

1.   Change over the previous period, 3-month moving average (s.a.a.r).
Source: Datastream; OECD.

Mexico, an order of magnitude is provided by the estimates carried out in 2001 for 22 other OECD countries. For these countries, where the problem might be more urgent because of their demographic structure, age-related spending (including pensions and health care for the elderly, etc.) is projected to increase by 6-7% of GDP over the next 50 years or so (starting from a spending ratio of close to 20% of GDP on average in 2000).

Another important positive development in Mexico is the move towards greater transparency in public accounts and budget management, especially after 1997, when the government in place ceased to have absolute majority in Congress.

The budget's dependency on oil-related revenue

Despite the positive developments listed above, there are still a number of weaknesses attached to fiscal policy. Rogelio Arellano and Fausto Hernández make the three following points: the tax base is narrow, oil-related revenue is volatile and, when there is a windfall gain ("oil bonus"), only a small proportion of it is allocated to the stabilisation fund, while the rest is used to finance primarily current expenditure. The paper emphasises that Mexico should: *i*) rely less on oil revenue and more on taxes, *ii*) redirect a larger share of oil-related windfall gains to long-term capital expenditure, and *iii*) increase the amounts saved into the stabilisation fund.

Figure 6.10. **Public sector budget balance and oil-related revenue**

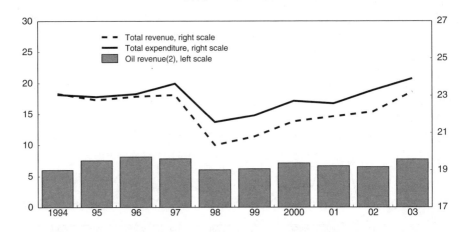

1.   The public sector comprises the federal government and the public enterprises under budget control (such as PEMEX). Financial intermediations by development banks is not included.
2.   Includes oil extractions royalties, VAT and excised taxes on oil products.
Source: Ministry of Finance, PEMEX.

Mexico's dependency on oil-related revenue is indeed very high, with about one-third of total revenue related to oil, and oil revenue is volatile (Figure 6.10). It is difficult to disagree with the recommendations made in the chapter, but I would add the following remarks:

- To meet essential development demands (human and infrastructure capital, poverty alleviation, etc.), higher spending levels are desirable and a higher quality of services is required.

- The distinction between current and capital expenditure is not always the most relevant. For instance, the largest part of spending on education is recorded as current expenditure, while it is really for human capital development.

- When windfall revenues are transferred to the states to finance outlays on infrastructure (according to the rules established in the budget every year), the cost-efficiency of additional spending is questionable, unless projects are incorporated in a medium-term investment planning framework.

CHALLENGES TO FISCAL ADJUSTMENT IN LATIN AMERICA – ISBN 9264022074 © OECD 2006

Thus, the key recommendations are: *i*) to improve the cost-efficiency of spending (especially in education), and *ii*) to frame spending programmes in a medium-term perspective (especially infrastructure).

The role of the Oil Stabilisation Fund

The high dependency on volatile revenue brings us to the role that the Oil Stabilisation Fund should play and the rules under which it should operate. This role depends heavily on the oil price set as a reference in the budget and, at this point in time, this price assumption is negotiated each year (Figure 6.11). A case may be made for setting the reference price of oil based on medium-term estimations. There should be an open discussion in Mexico on the issue. Then, once a benchmark has been set, a proportion of the windfall gains would be transferred to the stabilisation fund when the oil price moves much above this benchmark, and the reverse when the price falls below the benchmark.

Strengthening tax collection

Here again one can only agree with the chapter's recommendation that a tax reform is needed in Mexico, as illustrated in Figure 6.12. Some tax measures have been taken over the past but they fall short of what is needed. There is clearly room to widen the tax base while lowering tax rates.[13] This

Figure 6.11. **Oil prices and budget assumptions**

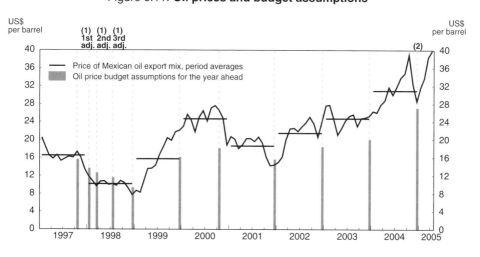

1. Adjustments made to the 1998 budget assumptions.
2. According to the budget proposal for 2005.
Source: Ministry of Finance; PEMEX.

Figure 6.12. **Tax revenue and the level of income in selected countries**[1]

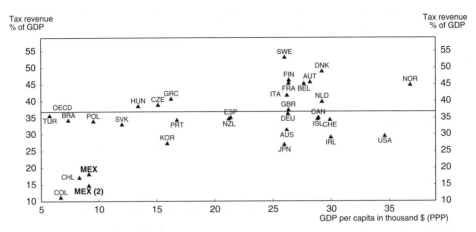

Tax revenue
% of GDP

Tax revenue
% of GDP

GDP per capita in thousand $ (PPP)

1. 2001 or nearest year available. Including social security contributions.
    Unweighted average for OECD.
2. Excluding PEMEX contributions to the federal government.
Source: OECD (2002), Revenue Statistics 1965-2001; OECD, National Accounts; Inter-American Center of Tax Administrations; World Bank.

would allow for an increase in tax revenue, while reducing the tax distortions and loopholes in the tax code that facilitate evasion. Everyone in Mexico agrees that a tax reform is needed, but disagrees on what to do and on how to do it, and nobody wants to pay the political cost of reform. However, the debate will not go away.

Pro-cyclicality of fiscal policy

As noted in the paper, the pro-cyclicality of fiscal policy remains a problem in Mexico, as in many other Latin American countries. The authors focus on measuring the appropriate indicator of the fiscal policy stance and to evaluate its impact on demand, and hence on inflation. It would also be interesting to measure the real effort at fiscal consolidation made by the government through discretionary action. This is what calculations of "structural fiscal indicators" made at the OECD for a number of its member-countries aim to do.[14]

Setting fiscal policy in a medium-term framework

Against this background, I would like to stress the need to set fiscal policy in a medium-term framework. This requires establishing medium-term projections that are updated regularly. Some important steps have been taken over the past few years, and this effort should continue. Among the benefits to be gained are that medium-term programming would help to reduce uncertainties about policy orientation; it would also allow the public debate to focus on longer-term policy priorities, rather than on cyclical developments, as is often the case during the annual budget discussion. A longer-term perspective is all the more important because of the public spending requirements that can strengthen growth over time, and these items (infrastructure, social spending, etc.) should not be subject to sharp adjustments from one year to the next. Many other OECD countries have incorporated forward projections in budget planning. Some Latin American countries also have medium-term fiscal rules. This is still lacking in Mexico.

Concluding remarks

Another dimension can be added to the fiscal challenges discussed by Rogelio Arellano and Fausto Hernández: the need to get the most out of public sector decentralisation. As Mexico moves ahead in decentralisation, it will have to redesign fiscal relations and address a number of issues, including maintaining fiscal control, ensuring administrative capacity at the state and local levels, and reviewing the rules for the allocation of resources to avoid horizontal imbalances among the states and municipalities.[15] In this context, an important issue is how much redistribution should be carried out through federal transfers to the states. Rogelio Arellano and Fausto Hernández looked at how much distribution is achieved through spending programmes at the national level. Fiscal federalism arrangements can influence these outcomes.

Notes

1.   Fiscal discipline was maintained even in electoral years, 1994 and 2000.

2.   The terms Ricardian (monetary dominance) and non-Ricardian (fiscal dominance) regimes were coined by Woodford (1995), in what became known as the fiscal theory of the price level (FTPL). The FTPL argues that the government's inter-temporal budget constraint is an equilibrium condition that determines the general price level, rather than an accounting identity. Advocates of this theory include Dupor (2000) and Sims (1994). For a detailed analysis of the FTPL, see Christiano and Fitzgerald (2000). However, Buiter (1997, 2004), Carlstrom and Fuerst (2000), Kocherlakota

and Phelan (1999) and McCallum (2003) are skeptical about the premises of the FTPL.

3.   This has been interpreted as a medium-term objective of budgetary positions close to balance or in surplus, but allows normal cyclical fluctuations while keeping the government deficit within 3% of GDP and the general government gross debt below 60% of GDP. For more information, see Balasonne and Franco (2001), Balasonne and Monacelli (2000), Canzoneri *et al.* (2002) and Gali and Peroti (2003).

4.   Notice, however, that fiscal rules in Latin America may not operate as effectively as the ones in the European Union due to weaker institutions. See Guidoti (2002) for further discussion.

5.   The government pays for its contracted obligations using the revenue generated by the project. From this perspective, the public-private partnership should be budget-neutral. However, the private sector partner does not bear the full risks associated with the project. As a result, it enjoys a preferential treatment concerning future disbursements, which may create a contingent liability for the budget.

6.   Santaella (2001) and CIDE-ITAM (2003) apply this methodology to the case of Mexico. The estimates reported below are based on an update of the calculations and include the recognition of new contingent liabilities that have arisen since then. Solis and Villagómez (1999) test for fiscal sustainability in Mexico using the methodology proposed by Uctum and Wickens (1996) and conclude that fiscal policy was sustainable during 1980-1997. Their estimates do not consider all the contingent liabilities that have arisen since then.

7.   Hernández *et al.* (2001) have shown that the Mexican federal government has a long tradition of bailing out the states, which may put federal fiscal balances in danger.

8.   All variables were estimated to be integrated of order 1. The Augmented Dickey Fuller tests are available upon request.

9.   The operational balance is defined as the primary balance minus real interest payments.

10.   See the Annex 6.1 for more information on the calculation of the EOB for Mexico.

CHALLENGES TO FISCAL ADJUSTMENT IN LATIN AMERICA – ISBN 9264022074 © OECD 2006

11. This is obtained by dividing VAT revenue (as a share of GDP) by the tax rate. South Korea's VAT productivity is 0.35, although its VAT code also has many different rates.

12. For more information, see World Bank (2004).

13. Specific recommendations have been made in OECD (1999). A reasonable benchmark would be to raise tax revenue by about 2% of GDP.

14. Calculations of structural fiscal indicators have also been made by the IMF (*cf.* Mexico: *Selected issues* 2001, IMF Country report no. 01/191, 2001). The calculations are based on public accounting data. It would be useful to calculate structural indicators based on consolidated general government accounts (national accounts definition). This is the kind of work carried out by the OECD for several of its member-countries, but not Mexico yet, a case where adjustments would need to be made for the impact of oil price changes.

15. This would include not only the quantitative aspects (*i.e.* amounts transferred to states), on which discussions are usually focused, but also issues such as how much control should be exerted by the central government, and how to monitor the quality of the services provided.

Bibliography

Ahmed, S. and J.H. Rogers (1995), "Government Budget Deficits and Trade Deficits: Are Present-Value Constraints Satisfied in Long-Term Data?", *Journal of Monetary Economics*, Vol. 36, pp. 351-74.

Balassone, F. and D. Franco (2001), "EMU Fiscal Rules: A New Answer to an Old Question", in *Fiscal Rules*, Banca d'Italia, Rome, pp. 33-58.

Balassone, F. and D. Manacelli (2000), "EMU Fiscal Rules: Is There a Gap?", Papers 375, Banca Italia, Rome.

Blejer, M. and A. Cheasty (1991), "The Measurement of Fiscal Deficits: Analytical and Methodological Issues", *Journal of Economic Literature*, Vol. 29, No. 4, pp. 1644-78.

Buiter, W.H. (1990), *Principles of Budgetary and Financial Policy*, MIT Press, Cambridge, MA.

Buiter, W. (1997), "Aspects of Fiscal Performance in some Transition Economies under Fund-Supported Programs", *International Monetary Fund Working Paper*, No. 97/31, IMF, Washington, D.C.

Buiter, W. (2004), "A Small Corner of Intertemporal Public Finance. New Developments in Monetary Economics: Two Ghosts, Two Eccentricities, a Fallacy, a Mirage and a Mythos". *CEPR Discussion Paper*, No. 4407, CEPR, London.

Canzoneri, M., R. Cumby and B. Diba (2002), "Should the European Central Bank and the Federal Reserve Be Concerned about Fiscal Policy?", Paper presented at the Federal Reserve Bank of Kansas City's Symposium on Rethinking Stabilization Policies, August, Jackson Hole, WY.

Carlstrom, C. and T. Fuerst (2000), "The Fiscal Theory of the Price Level", *Economic Review*, Federal Reserve Bank of Cleveland, Vol. 36, No. 1, pp. 22–32.

Christiano, L. and T. Fitzgerald (2000), "Understanding the Fiscal Theory of the Price Level" *Economic Review*, Federal Reserve Bank of Cleveland, Vol. 36, No. 2, pp. 1-38.

CIDE and ITAM (2003), *Análisis de las Finanzas Públicas en México*. Editado por Foro Consultivo de la Ciencia y el Consejo de Ciencia y Tecnología, México City.

Dalsgaard, T. (2000), "The Tax System in Mexico: A Need for Strengthening the Revenue-Raising Capacity", *OECD Economics Department Working Paper*, ECO/WKP(2000)6, OECD, Paris.

Dávila, E., S. Levy and G. Kessel (2001), "El sur También Existe: Un Ensayo sobre el Desarrollo Regional de México", *Economía Mexicana Nueva Epoca*, Vol. 11, No. 2, pp. 205-60.

Dupor, B. (2000), "Exchange Rates and the Fiscal Theory of the Price Level", *Journal of Monetary Economics*, Vol. 45, No. 3, pp. 613–30.

Easterly, W. and L. Servén (eds.) (2003), *The Limits of Stabilization: Infrastructure, Public Deficits, and Growth in Latin America*, Stanford University Press and World Bank.

Gali, J. and R. Perotti (2003), "Fiscal Policy and Monetary Integration in Europe", *NBER Working Papers*, No. 9773, NBER, Cambridge, MA.

Guidotti, P. (2002), "On Fiscal Rules in Latin America", Presented at the IMF/World Bank Conference on Rules-Based Fiscal Policy in Emerging Market Economies, Oaxaca, Mexico.

Hamilton, J. and Y M. Flavin (1986), "On the Limitations of Government Borrowing: A Framework for Empirical Testing", *American Economic Review*, Vol. 76, No. 4, pp. 808-19.

Hernández Trillo, F., A. Díaz C. and R. Gamboa (2001), "Bailing-out States in Mexico", *Eastern Economic Journal*, Vol. 28, No. 3, pp. 365-80.

Hernandez Trillo, F. and A. Zamudio C. (2004), *Evasión Fiscal en México: el caso del IVA*. Sistema de Administración Tributaria, México City.

Kocherlakota, N. and C. Phelan (1999), "Explaining the Fiscal Theory of the Price Level", *Quarterly Review*, Federal Reserve Bank of Minneapolis, Vol. 23, No. 4, pp. 14-23.

Liviatan, N. (2003), "Fiscal Dominance and Monetary Dominance in the Israeli Monetary Experience", *Discussion Paper*, No. 2003.17, Bank of Israel, Jerusalem.

McCallum, B. (2003), "Is the Fiscal Theory of the Price Level Learnable?", *NBER Working Paper*, No. 9961, NBER, Cambridge, MA.

OECD (1999), *Economic Survey of Mexico*, OECD, Paris.

Santaella, J. (2001), "La Viabilidad de la Política Fiscal: 2000–2025", *Gaceta de Economía,* Special issue Una Agenda para las Finazas Públicas de México, ITAM, pp. 37-65.

Scott, J. (2004), "Algunas Consideraciones Sobre la Incidencia del Gasto Social en México". *Documento de Trabajo*, CIDE, Mexico City.

Sims, C. (1994), "A Simple Model for the Study of the Determination of the Price Level and the Interaction of Monetary and Fiscal Policy", *Economic Theory*, Vol. 4, No. 3, pp. 381-99.

Solís, F. and A. Villagómez (1999), "La Sustentabilidad de la Política Fiscal en México", *El Trimestre Económico*, Vol. 66, No. 4.

Talvi, E. and C. Végh (2000), "La Viabilidad de la Política Fiscal: Un modelo Macro Básico", in E. Talvi and C. Végh (eds.), *¿Cómo Armar el Rompecabezas Fiscal? Nuevos Indicadores de Sosteniblidad*, Inter-American Development Bank, Washington, D.C.

Uctum, M. and M. Wickens (1996), "Debt and Deficit Ceilings, and Sustainability of Fiscal policies: An Intertemporal Analysis", *Research Paper*, No. 9615, Federal Reserve Bank of New York, New York, NY.

Wilcox, D. (1989), "The Sustainability of Government Deficit: Implications of the Present Value Constraint", *Journal of Money, Credit and Banking*, Vol. 21, pp. 291-306.

World Bank (2004), Mexico Public Expenditure Review, Mimeo, World Bank, Washington, D.C.

Woodford, M. (1995), "Price Level Determinacy without Control of a Monetary Aggregate", *Carnegie-Rochester Series on Public Policy*, Vol. 43, pp. 1-46.

Woodford, M. (2001), "Fiscal Requirements for Price Stability", *NBER Working Paper*, No. 8072, NBER, Cambridge, MA.

Annex 6.1

Fiscal sustainability and the expanded operational balance

Testing for fiscal sustainability

Talvi and Végh (2000) use a one-period public-sector budget constraint (the possibility of money creation is omitted for algebraic simplicity):

$$B_t - (1+i)B_{t-1} = G_t - Z_t \qquad (1)$$

where B_t denotes the stock of public debt at time t, G_t is public expenditure at time t, Z_t is total revenue at t, i is the (constant) nominal interest rate between periods $t\text{-}1$ and t.

Equation (1) can be re-written as shares of GDP as:

$$\tilde{b}_t = \left(\frac{1+r}{1+\theta}\right)\tilde{b}_{t-1} + \tilde{g}_t - \tilde{z}_t \qquad (2)$$

where lower-case letters denote real variables, a tilde denotes variables expressed as shares of GDP, the real interest rate is defined as $r = [(1+i)/(1+\pi)] - 1$, and θ is the (constant) rate of growth of GDP.

Letting $\delta = \tilde{g}_t - \tilde{z}_t$ denote the primary deficit as a share of GDP, Equation (2) can be written as:

$$\tilde{b}_t = \left(\frac{1+r}{1+\theta}\right)\tilde{b}_{t-1} + \delta_t \qquad (3)$$

The government's inter-temporal budget constraint can then be computed by iterating forward Equation (3) up to n period, such that b_{t+n} can be expressed as:

CHALLENGES TO FISCAL ADJUSTMENT IN LATIN AMERICA – ISBN 9264022074 © OECD 2006

$$\left(\frac{1+\theta}{1+r}\right)^n \tilde{b}_{t+n} = \left(\frac{1+r}{1+\theta}\right)\tilde{b}_{t-1} + \sum_{j=0}^{n}\left(\frac{1+\theta}{1+r}\right)^j \delta_{t+j} \qquad (4)$$

For a large n, and assuming that $r>\theta$, the LHS tends to zero and implies that government debt must be equal to zero in a present value sense. Hence, Equation (4) may be rewritten as:

$$\tilde{b}_{t-1} = -\sum_{j=0}^{\infty}\left(\frac{1+\theta}{1+r}\right)^{j+1} \delta_{t+j} \qquad (5)$$

Equation (5) indicates that the present discounted value of net revenues (RHS) must equal the initial stock of government debt. Talvi and Végh (2000) argue that δ is a path that satisfies Equation (5), thus defining a permanent primary deficit, δ^*, as the constant level of the primary balance whose present discounted value in t is equal to the present discounted value of the path of actual primary balances:

$$\sum_{j=0}^{\infty}\left(\frac{1+\theta}{1+r}\right)^j \delta_t^* = \sum_{j=0}^{\infty}\left(\frac{1+\theta}{1+r}\right)^j \delta_{t+j} \qquad (6)$$

Solving for δ^* and substituting Equation (6) into Equation (5) yields:

$$-\delta^* = \left[\frac{r-\theta}{1+r}\right]\tilde{b}_{t-1} \qquad (7)$$

Equation (7) is the condition for debt sustainability: the primary surplus $(-\delta^*)$ must equate the effective real interest payments on the initial stock of government debt. Clearly, fiscal policy is unsustainable if this equation is greater than zero and sustainable otherwise.

Calculation of the expanded operational balance (EOB)

The EOB includes on the expenditure side: domestic purchases of goods and services, both by the federal government and the state-owned enterprises (including off-budget operations and the sub-national governments' expenditure linked to federal revenue-sharing programmes); transfers to households or individuals; total investment in buildings, domestic equipment and machinery, including off-budget investment projects (PIDIREGAS); the real component of domestic interest payments, including transfers to the deposit insurance fund

(IPAB) and debtor relief programmes (ADE);[1] and payments to be made in the following fiscal year (Adefas).

On the revenue side, the EOB includes: taxes, non-oil duties and domestic oil duties (*i.e.* excludes oil duties paid by foreigners), social security contributions, and federal domestic sales of goods and services (including off-budget operations).

Finally, the financial intermediation of development banks and public trust funds is also included due to the fact that credit granted by these institutions may not reflect market conditions and is earmarked for sectors that, given the high risk associated with their investment projects, would only have access to credits at very high rates or, indeed, no access at all. On the other hand, the Ministry of Finance has traditionally published the economic and the primary balances originally pursuing a similar end.

Note

1. This is obtained by subtracting the inflationary adjustment of the principal from nominal interest payments.

CHALLENGES TO FISCAL ADJUSTMENT IN LATIN AMERICA – ISBN 9264022074 © OECD 2006

OECD PUBLICATIONS, 2, rue André-Pascal, 75775 PARIS CEDEX 16
PRINTED IN FRANCE
(11 2006 03 1 P) ISBN 92-64-02207-4 – No. 55005 2006

4803 71